5000 Babies' Names

5000 Babies' Names

ROBERT HALE · LONDON

First published in Great Britain 2010

ISBN 978-0-7090-9108-0

Robert Hale Limited
Clerkenwell House
Clerkenwell Green
London EC1R 0HT

www.halebooks.com

A catalogue record for this book is available from the British Library

2 4 6 8 10 9 7 5 3 1

Typeset by e-type, Liverpool
Printed in Great Britain by
CPI Bookmarque

ABBREVIATIONS RELATING TO ORIGINAL SOURCES OF NAMES

Ang.-Sax.	Anglo-Saxon	Jap.	Japanese
Arab.	Arabian	Lat.	Latin
Arm.	Armenian	Lit.	Lithuanian
Celt.	Celtic	Man.	Mandaean
Chin.	Chinese	N.A. Ind.	North American Indian
Dan.	Danish		
Eng.	English	Nor.	Norse
Egyp.	Egyptian	Old Eng.	Old English
Finn.	Finnish	Old Fr.	Old French
Flem.	Flemish	Pers.	Persian
Fr.	French	Pho.	Phoenician
Frie.	Friesian	Rus.	Russian
Gael.	Gaelic	Sans.	Sanskrit
Gr.	Greek	Scan.	Scandinavian
Haw.	Hawaiian	Slav.	Slavonic
Her.	Hebrew	Span.	Spanish
Hin.	Hindustani	Sud.	Sudani
Hung.	Hungarian	Teut.	Teutonic
Ice.	Icelandic	Turk.	Turkish
It.	Italian	Wel.	Welsh

GIRLS' NAMES

A

AASTA: (Teut.) love
ABDULIA: (Span.) certain
ABHA: (Hin.) lustrous
ABIGAIL: (Arab.) father's joy; (Heb.) father of joy
ABIRA: (Heb.) strong
ABNAKI: (N.A. Ind.) morning land
ABRONA: (Lat.) goddess of departures
ACACIA: (Gr.) guileless; innocent
ACADIA: (N.A. Ind.) place of plenty
ACANTHA: (Gr.) thorny
ACIMA: (Heb.) the Lord will judge
ACOLA: (Teut.) cool
ACTIA: (Gr.) ray of light
ADA: (Teut.) happy
ADABEL: (Teut.-Lat.) happy one
ADAH: (Heb.) ornament
ADALIA: (Gr.) not easily understood
ADAMINA: (Heb.) of the earth, mortal; also feminine Scottish form of Adam
ADAR: (Heb.) fire; a Hebrew calendar period
ADARA: (Gr.) a virgin
ADELAIDE: (Teut.) noble, princess
ADELINE: (Teut.) of noble bearing or lineage
ADELLBERTA: (Teut.) nobly bright
ADELPHE: (Gr.) beloved sister
ADENA: (Gr.) accepted; (Teut.) noble
ADERYN: (Wel.) bird
ADICIA: (Lat.) unjustly treated; (Gr.) injustice
ADIEL: (Heb.) ornament of the Lord
ADIN: (Heb.) slender; delicate

ADINA: (Heb.) slender; voluptuous
ADIONE: (Lat.) a Roman divinity who presides over movements of travellers
ADIRA: (Heb.) strong
ADITI: (Hin.) free
ADNAH: (Heb.) pleasure
ADONICA: (Lat.) sweet
ADORA: (Lat.) one adored; (Gr.) a gift
ADOSINDA: (Teut.) of great strength
ADRA: (Span.) in turn
ADRANA: (Gr.) a girl from Ardrea
ADRIANNE: feminine form of Adrian
ADRIENNE: (see Adrianne)
AELWEN: (Wel.) fair brow
AENEA: (Heb.) praiseworthy
AERON: (Celt.) bright queen
AERONA: (Wel.) like a berry
AERONWEN: (Wel.) fair berry
AFRA: (Teut.) peaceful ruler; (Heb.) dust
AGADA: (Sans.) healthy
AGALIA: (Gr.) restless
AGATHA: (Gr.) good
AGEE: (Heb.) one who flees
AGILA: (Lat.) active in mind and body
AGNELLA: (Gr.) pure
AGNES: (Lat.) lamb, denoting gentleness; (Gr.) chaste, pure
AGNOLA: (Lat.) an angel
AGOKAY: (N.A. Ind.) persevering
AGOLA: (Span.) woman who handles the sails
AGRIPPINA: (Lat.) born feet foremost
AH-CY: (Chin.) lovely
AHIMSA: (Hin.) virtuous
AH-KEM: (Chin.) good as gold
AH-LAM: (Chin.) orchid-like
AILEEN: an Irish form of Helen or Helene, from (Gr.) light
AILSA: (Gael.) undiscoverable; a Scottish form of Elsa
AIMEE: (Fr.) beloved
AINA: (Scottish) own

AISHA: (Arab.) lively
AISLINN: (Celt.) dream or vision
AKALA: (Haw.) respected
AKI: (Jap.) autumn
ALA: (Teut.) holy
ALAME, ALAMEDA: (Span.) like the stately poplar tree
ALANA: (Celt.) my child
ALANIS: (Fr.) shining star
ALATEA: (see Althea)
ALBA: (Lat.) white
ALBERTA: feminine form of Albert
ALBERTINA: (Ang.-Sax.) bright or illustrious; feminine form of Albert
ALBINA, ALBINIA: (Lat.) white
ALCINA: (Gr.) sea-maiden
ALCYONE: (Gr.) calm
ALDA: (Teut.) happy, rich
ALDIS: (Old Eng.) from the old house
ALDITH, ALDYTH: (Old Eng.) old battle
ALDORA: (Gr.) winged gift
ALEA: (Arab.) excellent
ALESHIA: (Gr.) honest
ALESSA: (It.) helper
ALETHA: (Gr.) truth
ALETTA: (Lat.) winged, little wing; (Gr.) carefree
ALEXANDRA, ALEXANDRINA: (Gr.) help of men; feminine form of Alexander
ALEXIA: (Teut.) German form of Alexandra, from (Gr.) help of men
ALFREDA: (Teut.-Ang.-Sax.) wise counsel
ALIA: (Arab.) girl of the sky
ALICE: believed to have evolved from German (Adelaide) and Old French (Aliz); in Latinized form meaning noble or a princess
ALICIA: a nineteenth-century romanticized form of Alice
ALINA: (Lat.) in a straight line
ALINE: (Teut.) noble; evolved from Adeline
ALISHA: (Gr.) truthful; happy
ALISON: (Teut.) a famous war-maid; (Gr.) flower of the Alyssum family

ALLEGRA: (It.) cheerful; comforter
ALMA: (Lat.) benign or loving; (Sans.) spirit mind
ALMEIDA: (Span.) shining
ALMETA: (Lat.) forward to the goal; brisk and industrious
ALMIRA: (Arab.) the exalted one, princess; (Hin.) a receptacle for clothing
ALODIA, ALODIE: (Lat.-Teut.) wealth; a prosperous woman
ALOYSIA: (Teut.) famous war-maid; feminine form of Aloysius
ALPHA: (Gr.) first
ALPHONSINE: (Teut.) nobly ready and eager for war
ALTHEA: (Gr.) from Alethea, meaning truth
ALUDRA: (Gr.) a virgin
ALVA, ALVINA: (Lat.) the sedge; (Span.) white
ALVARA: (Port.) white
ALVINA: (Teut.) elfin friend
ALVIRA: (Teut.) elfin arrow
ALVITA: (Lat.-Teut.) full of life, vivacious
ALYSIA: (Gr.) a chain; unbroken bond; possessive
ALYSSA: (Gr.) a flower name; probably derived from Alysson, a plant reputed to cure madness
ALZENA: (Arab.) woman
AMABEL, AMABELLA, AMABELLE: (Lat.) loved one; lovable creature
AMADEA: (Lat.) loving God, to love God
AMALABERTA: (Teut.) bright worker
AMALBURGA: (Teut.) a bright nature
AMALIA: (Hung.) industrious
AMANDA: (Lat.) lovable
AMANTA: (Lat.) loving
AMARA: (Sans.) immortal
AMARANTHA: (Gr.) unfading (as a flower)
AMARIS: (Heb.) the promised one; (Lat.) child of the moon
AMARYLLIS: (Gr.)

refreshing stream; (Lat.) a country girl

AMBER: (Arab.) originally from Ambergris, now applied to yellowish fossil resin; the yellow one

AMBROSINE: (Gr.) immortal; feminine form of Ambrose

AMELIA: (Gr.) energetic

AMELIE: French form of Amelia

AMELINA, AMELITA: (Gr.) energetic; derivatives of Amelia

AMENA: (Celt.) honest

AMETHYST: (Lat.) sobering; (Gr.) the sober one. A quartz anciently supposed to prevent drunkenness

AMIA: (Ger.) beloved

AMILIA: a Scottish form of Emily

AMINE: (Arab.) faithful

AMINTA: (Gr.) protection

AMITY: (Lat.) friendship

AMORET, AMORETTE: (Lat.) little darling, sweetheart; a love-knot. Related to Italian 'amoretto' and French 'amour'

AMORITA: (Lat.) she who is beloved

AMY: (Lat.) loved one

AMYNTAS: (Gr.) helper

ANALEESE: (Scan.) gracious

ANASTASIA: (Gr.) resurrection

ANATOLA: (Gr.) sunrise

ANCELIN: (Lat.) servant; handmaid

ANCITA: (Heb.) grace

ANDEANA: (Span.) walker; a goer

ANDREA: (Gr.) brave

ANDREANA: (Gr.) a man's woman

ANDROMEDA: (Gr.) man-ruler. In mythology princess rescued by Perseus

ANEIRA: (Wel.) truly white or truly golden

ANEMONE: (Gr.) frail wind flower

ANGELA: (Gr.) angelic

ANGELICA: (Lat.) messenger of the angels

ANGELINA, ANGELINE: (see Angela)

ANGHARAD: (Wel.) graceful
ANGWEN, ANNWEN: (Wel.) very beautiful
ANIELA: angel; from Italian Angelo
ANITA: (Heb.) little Ann
ANN: (Heb.) grace
ANNA, ANNE: (see Ann)
ANNABEL: (Heb.-Lat.) beautiful Anna; also formed of two words, Anna (grace) and Bella (fair)
ANNABELLA, ANNABELLE: variants of Annabel
ANNETTE: French form of Anne
ANNONA: (Lat.) fruitful one
ANNORA: (Heb.) grace, as with Ann
ANNYS: (Gr.) complete
ANSELMA: (Teut.) divine protectress
ANTHEA: (Gr.) flowery; lady of flowers
ANTHELIA: (Gr.) opposite the sun
ANTOINETTE: (Gr.) a girl in bloom
ANTONIA: (Lat.) inestimable
ANWYL: (Wel.) dear
ANYA: (Rus.) grace
ANYSIA: (Gr.) complete
ANZONETTA: (Teut.) little one of divine origin
APRIL: (Lat.) the fertile one; to open as nature in spring
AQUILA: (Lat.) eagle
AQUILINA: (Lat.) little eagle
ARA: (Lat.) an altar
ARABELLA: (Teut.) beautiful eagle
ARAMINTA: origin obscure; probably a conjunction of 'ara' (altar) and 'moneta' (coinage of money). A free translation would be sacred coinage
ARCADIA: (Gr.) ideal land of peace, happiness and beauty
ARDANA: (Sans.) restless
ARDATH: (Heb.) flowering field
ARDDUN: (Wel.) sublime
ARDELIA: (Lat.) zealous

ARDINE: (Gr.) she who satisfies. From the word meaning to water, to quench

ARDIS: (Lat.) ardent gratifier

ARDRA: (Lat.) she who is ardent, or desirous

ARETA: (Gr.) maiden of virtue

ARETHUSA: (Gr.) virtuous. In mythology a nymph who was saved from her pursuers by being changed into a fountain

ARIADNE: (Gr.) sweet singer

ARIANA: (Lat.-Heb.) song of grace

ARIANWEN: (Wel.) silvery-white

ARIEL: (Heb.) lion of God; sometimes referred to as the spirit of air, as in *The Tempest* by Shakespeare

ARIELLA: (Heb.) hearth of God

ARISTA: (Gr.) wonderful

ARLEEN, ARLENE: (Teut.) a pledge

ARMILDA: (Teut.) armed battle-maid

ARMILLA, ARMIL: (Lat.) bracelet, armlet

ARMILLETTE: (Lat.) the gentle embracer; derived from 'armilla', meaning bracelet or armlet

ARMINE, ARMINEL: (Ang.-Sax.) universal

ARMOREL: (Gael.) dweller by the sea

ARNHILDA: (Teut.) eagle battle-maid

ARNOLDINE: (Teut.) the eagle's mate

ARTEMA: (Gr.) moon goddess

ARTEMISIA: (Gr.) perfect one

ARVA: (Teut.) lofty powers

ASHER: (Heb.) blessed

ASHLEY, ASHLEIGH: (Eng.) a woodland sprite; from a woodland field

ASPASIA: (Gr.) radiant as a star

ASTA: (Teut.) swift as the wolf

ASTRA, ASTREA: (Gr.) shining star

ASTRED: (Gr.) the starry one
ASTRELLA, ASTRELLITA: (Gr.) little star
ASTRID: (Nor.) godly strength
ATALANTA: (Gr.) delicate huntress
ATALIE: (Scan.) innocent maiden
ATHALIA, ATHALIAH: (Heb.) God is mighty and exalted
ATHENA: (Gr.) a woman of wisdom
ATHENE: (Gr.) goddess of wisdom; goddess of Athens
AUBERTA: (Teut.) bright, fair girl; a variant of Alberta
AUDREY: (Teut.) regal counsellor
AUGUSTA: (Lat.) revered; feminine form of Augustine
AURA: (Gr.) gentle wind, breeze
AUREA: (Lat.) golden
AURELIA: (Lat.) the golden one
AUREOLA: (Lat.) golden
AURORA, AURORE: (Lat.) dawn
AUTUMN: (Lat.) joy in the changing seasons
AVA: (Lat.) pretty one
AVELINE: (Heb.) pleasantness
AVERIL: (Fr.) month of April; name of a seventh-century Yorkshire saint
AVERY: (Fr.) flirtatious
AVIS: (Teut.) a refugee in trouble; also a gipsy name
AVISSA: (Lat.) maiden of bird-like delicacy
AVONWY: (Wel.) dweller by the river
AWEL: (Wel.) breeze, zephyr
AYESHA: (Pers.) happy
AYLWEN: (Wel.) fair of brow
AZALIA: (Gr.) dry; also name of flower
AZARIA: (Heb.) blessed of God
AZARINE: (Teut.) noble woman
AZURA: (Arab.-Pers.) blue

B

BABETTE: (Gr.) little Barbara
BAHIR: (Arab.) striking
BAILEY: (Eng.) bailiff; berry clearing
BAPTISTA, BATISTA: (Gr.) baptized (in the Lord's name)
BARBARA: (Gr.) the stranger
BARBETTE: (Gr.) little stranger
BARIKA: (Heb.) chosen one
BASSANIA: (Gr.) of the deep-sea realm
BATHILDA: (Teut.) commanding maid of battle
BATHSHEBA: (Heb.) daughter of the oath
BEATA: (Lat.) blessed
BEATRICE, BEATRIX: (Lat.) one who blesses; happiness; bringer of joy
BECHIRA: (Heb.) the chosen child
BEILA: (Span.) beautiful
BEKA: (Heb.) half-sister
BELA: (Hung.) nobly; (Heb.) God's earth
BELDA: (Old Fr.) beautiful woman; (Teut.) good mother
BELINDA: (Lat.) sinuous like a serpent
BELLA, BELLE: (It.-Fr.) beautiful; Scottish diminutive of Isabel
BELVINA: (Lat.) fair one
BENA: (Heb.) wise; (N.A. Ind.) the pheasant
BENEDICTA, BENICE: (Lat.) she who is blessed
BENITA: (Lat.) blessed one
BERENICE, BERNICE: (Gr.) bringer of victory
BERNADETTE: (Teut.) the courageous little one
BERNADINE: (Teut.) bold, masterful; feminine form of Bernard
BERNESSA: (Teut.) maid of the bear strain, from 'bera', meaning bear; valorous
BERNETTE: (Teut.) brave little maid

BERTHA: (Teut.) bright, or beautiful one
BERTHELDA: (Teut.) bright battle-maid
BERULE: (Gr.) bright; pure
BERYL: (Pers.) crystal; name of gemstone
BESS, BESSIE, BETH, BETSY: shortened forms of Elizabeth
BETHANEY: (Heb.) home of poverty; house of dates
BETHANY: (Heb.) disciple of God
BETHESDA: (Heb.) house of mercy
BEULAH: (Heb.) matronly; she who is married
BEVERLEY: variant of old English name Bevis
BIANCA: (Lat.) fair
BIBI: (Arab.) lady
BIDDY: (Celt.) a goddess; Irish contraction of Bridget
BILLIE: (Teut.) feminine form of William
BINA: (Heb.) knowledge
BLANCH: (Teut.) white
BLANCHE: French form of Blanch
BLANDA: (Lat.) flatterer
BLENDA: (Teut.) dazzling white
BLODEYN: (Wel.) flower
BLODWEN: (Wel.) flower-white
BLYTHE: (Ang.-Sax.) joyous, friendly
BONNIE, BONNY: (Ang.-Sax.) good; (Gael.) pretty, probably from the French 'bonne', meaning pretty one
BRANWEN, BRANGWIRIN: (Wel.) little raven
BRENDA: (Teut.) a flaming sword
BRENNA: (Celt.) the dark-haired; (Slav.) maiden with raven hair
BRIANA, BRIANNA: (Teut.) a flame; strong
BRIDGET, BRIGID: (Celt.) strong one
BRITTANY: (Lat.) from England
BRONWEN, BRONWYN: (Cymric) white breast
BRONYA: (Rus.) armour
BROOKE: (Eng.)

sophisticated; small stream
BRUNILDA, BRUNHILDE, BRYNHILD: (Teut.) compounded from 'brunnia' (corslet) and 'hill' (battle); breastplate or battle-maid
BRYONY: (Lat.) a clinging vine
BUENA: (Span.) good
BURNETTA: (Old Fr.) little brown one

C

CABIN: (Lat.) keel
CABRIOLE: (Fr.) adorable
CADY: (Eng.) fun-loving
CAITLIN: (Irish) virginal
CALANDRA: (Gr.) a lark
CALDORA: (Gr.) beautiful gift
CALLENA: (Teut.) talkative
CALLIDA: (Span.) warm, sincere
CALLIOPE: (Gr.) beautiful voice; muse of heroic poetry
CALLISTA: (Gr.) of great beauty
CALLUELLA: (Gr.) extremely beautiful
CALLULA: (Gr.) beauty
CALOSA: (Gr.) beautiful to behold
CALTHA: (Lat.) a marigold
CALVINA: (Lat.) bright-haired
CALYPSO: (Gr.) nymph of the sea
CAMELLIA: (It.) flower
CAMERON: (Gael.) bent nose; popular
CAMILLA: (Lat.) a freeborn attendant at a sacrifice
CAMILLE: (Gr.) a swift-footed messenger of Diana
CANDA: (Celt.-Wel.) brightness
CANDACE: (Lat.) glowing
CANDIDA: (Lat.) white
CANNA: (Lat.) a reed or cane; flower name
CAPELLA: (Lat.) a star in the constellation of Auriga
CAPRICE: (It.) playful
CARA: (Celt.) friend

CARESSE: (Gr.) much-loved
CARISSA: (Lat.) dear little schemer
CARITA: (Lat.) charity
CARLA: (Teut.) virile; diminutive form of Caroline, Carolyn
CARLETTA: (Teut.) little virile one
CARLOTTA: Italian form of Charlotte
CARME: (Gr.) in classic mythology, a nymph
CARMEL: (Heb.) a vineyard; (Arab.) a field of fruit
CARMELA: (Heb.) of the vineyard
CARMEN: (Heb.) crimson
CARMIA: (Lat.) rosy
CARMINE: (It.) attractive
CAROL: (Gael.) melody; popular in modern times (particularly in USA) as a shortened form of Caroline
CAROLINE, CAROLYN: (Teut.) virile
CARRIE: English contraction of Caroline
CASEY: (Irish) watchful, alert
CASILDA: (Span.) the solitary one
CASIMIRA: (Lat.) bearer of peace
CASSANDRA: (Gr.) one who excites love
CASSIA: (Gr.) the cassia tree
CASSIDY: (Irish) clever girl
CASSIOPEIA: (Gr.) fragrance of flowers; mother of Andromeda
CASTA, CASTARA: (Lat.) chaste
CATALINA: (Span.) a small parrot
CATHABELL: (Gr.-Lat.) pure beauty
CATHARINE, CATHERINE: (Gr.) pure, name of virgin martyr of Alexandria
CATHIE: Scottish diminutive of Catherine
CATHLEEN: (Irish) pure, immaculate
CATHLIN: (Celt.) beautiful eves
CATRIONA: probably a

Scottish variant of Catharine, from the Greek meaning pure
CATTIMA: (Lat.) slender reed
CAYLA: (Heb.) unblemished
CECILE, CECILIA, CECILY: variants of Celia
CEDRELA: (Lat.) the silver fir
CEIN: (Celt.) jewel
CELENA: (Gr.) dark
CELESTA, CELESTE, CELESTINE: (Lat.) heavenly
CELIA: (Lat.) heaven; sky
CELO: (Gr.) flaming
CELOSIA: (Gr.) aflame; name of flower
CENTELLA: (Lat.) flashing light
CERA: (Fr.) colourful; (Span.) growth
CERELIA: (Lat.) pertaining to Ceres, goddess of grain and harvests; fruitful woman
CERRITA: (Span.) closed; sealed lips
CERYLE: (Lat.) a sea bird
CERYS, CARYS: (Wel.) love
CHAI: (Heb.) life-giving
CHANDRA: (Sans.) a goddess brighter than the stars; destroyer of evil
CHANIA: (Heb.) blessed by the grace of the Lord
CHANTAL: (Fr.) one who sings
CHANTESUTA: (N.A. Ind.) firm of heart
CHAREMON: (Gr.) the spirit rejoicing
CHARIS: (Gr.) goodwill; in mythology one of the three graces
CHARITY: (Lat.) charitable; giver of love
CHARLOTTE: (Teut.-Fr.) virile, noble; feminine form of English Charles and Italian Carlo
CHARMA: (Gr.) delight, joy
CHARMAINE: (Lat.) little song
CHARMIAN: (Gr.) a little joy; Cleopatra's favourite serving maid
CHARO: (Span.) flower

CHASTINE: (Lat.) pure
CHAVVAH: (Heb.) giver of life
CHELSEA: (Old Eng.) safe harbour
CHENIA: (Heb.) she who lives by God's grace
CHENOA: (N.A. Ind.) white dove
CHER, CHERIE: (Fr.) dear
CHERRY: (Gr.) beloved
CHERYL: modern usage, probably from fiction
CHIARA: (It.) famous
CHILALI: (N.A. Ind.) snow-bird
CHIMALIS: (N.A. Ind.) blue-bird
CHIQUITA: (Span.) little
CHISPA: (Span.) a spark
CHITSA: (N.A. Ind.) fair one
CHLOE: (Gr.) a young green shoot, blooming
CHLORA: (Gr.) freshness of spring, verdure
CHLORINE: (Gr.) golden green
CHLORIS: (Gr.) blooming, fresh
CHO: (Jap.) butterfly
CHOLENA: (N.A. Ind.) bird
CHRESTELLA: (Gr.) good, worthy
CHRISTABEL: (Gr.) anointed one; fair follower of Christ
CHRISTEL: (Gr.) ice-like
CHRISTIANE: (Gr.) a Christian
CHRISTINE, CHRISTINA: (Lat.) messenger or follower of Christ
CHRYSILLA: (Gr.) golden-haired
CHUMA: (Heb.) warm
CHUN: (Chin.) spring
CIARA: (Irish) brown-haired
CICILY: (from Cecilia)
CLADONIA: (Gr.) a branch (of a tree or plant)
CLAIRINE: (Lat.) bright maid
CLARA: (Lat.) bright, clear
CLARE, CLAIRE: variants of Clara
CLARENDA: (Lat.) brightening
CLARESTA: (Lat.) bright glory

CLARETTE: (Lat.) little bright one
CLARIBEL: (Lat.) brightly fair
CLARICE, CLARISSA: variants of Clara
CLARIMOND: (Lat.) world-famed
CLARINITA: (Lat.) famous little one
CLAUDETTE: (Lat.) little lame one
CLAUDIA: (Lat.) lame
CLAUDINE: French form of Claudia
CLEANTHA: (Gr.) famous bloom
CLEARESTA: (Gr.) highest peak of glory
CLEINE: (Gr.) famous
CLEMATIS: (Gr.) lithe; flower name
CLEMENTINA, CLEMENTINE: (Lat.) merciful, gentle
CLEO: (Gr.) glorious
CLEODORA: (Gr.) glorious gift
CLEONIMIA: (Gr.) glorious name
CLEOPATRA: (Gr.) from a famous father
CLEOPHILA: (Gr.) lover of glory
CLEOSA: (Gr.) famous
CLEVA: (Lat.) a hilltop or cliff
CLORINDA: (Pers.) renowned
CLORIS: (Lat.) pale
CLOTHILDA, CLOTHILDE: (Teut.) battle-maid; compound of 'hloda' (loud) and 'hildi' (battle)
CLYDINA: (Gr.) glorious one
CLYMENIA: (Gr.) famous
CLYTE: (Gr.) in mythology, a maiden whom the gods turned into a sunflower – hence, looking to the sun
COCHETA: (N.A. Ind.) the unknown
COLINETTE: (Lat.) little dove
COLLEEN: (Irish) a girl
COLUMBIA: (Lat.) a dove
COLUMBINE: (Lat.) flower name

COMFORT: (Old Eng.) consolation, compassion. A name favoured by the Puritans
CONCEPTION: (Lat.) fruitful; sometimes used in honour of the Immaculate Conception
CONCESSA: (Lat.) granting of a favour
CONCETTA: (It.) an ingenious idea
CONCHA: (Lat.) a sea-shell
CONCORDIA: (Lat.) harmony; agreeable
CONNAL: (Lat.) faithful
CONRADINE: (Teut.) wise counsel
CONSTANCE: (Lat.) faithful, constant
CONSUELA, CONSUELO: (Lat.) one who consoles
CONTESSA: (It.) pretty
CORA: (Gr.) a maiden
CORAH: (Hin.) constant
CORAL: (Gr.) from the sea coral
CORALIE: (Fr.) coral, a modern French invention
CORDANA: (Teut.) harmonizing
CORDELIA: (Celt.) jewel of the sea; (Lat.) warm-hearted
CORETTA: (Gr.) little maiden
CORINNA: (Gr.) maiden
CORLA: (Old Eng.) the curlew
CORNELIA: (Lat.) enduring; feminine of Cornelius, meaning hornlike
COROLLA: (Lat.) a small crown
CORONA: (Gr.) a crown
CORRA: (Celt.) a mountain glen
COSETTE: (Teut.) a pet lamb
COTTINA: (Gr.) crown of wild flowers
COULAVA: (Celt.) soft-handed
COURTNEY, COURTENEY: (Eng.) domain of Curtius
COYETTA: (Teut.) caged
COYNE: (Old Fr.) reserved, modest
CRESENTIA: (Lat.) of the half-moon

CRESSA: (Teut.) water-cress
CRESSIDA: (Gr.) faithlessness
CRISPINA: (Lat.) curly-headed. Probably from 'crispus', meaning curled
CRISTY: (Lat.) the anointed
CYBILL: (Lat.) prophetess
CYNTHIA: (Gr.) of, or from, Mt Cynthus, signifying lofty
CYRA: (Gr.) lady
CYRENE: (Gr.) a river nymph
CYRILLA: (Lat.) royal

D

DABARATH, DABERATH: (Heb.) from a cool part
DACIA: (Lat.) from afar
DAFFODIL: (Gr.) flower name of the lily family, especially the Asphodel
DAGMAR: (Teut.) Dane's glory
DAGNA: (Teut.) radiant as the day
DAHLIA: (Scan.) flower name
DAINA: (Teut.) disdainful
DAISY: (Pers.) brightness; (Ang.-Sax.) day's eve. Also late-Victorian pet-name for Margaret
DAI-TAI: (Chin.) lead-boy. In Chinese families of many girls where a boy is hoped for, this name is given to a daughter in the belief that she will be followed by a brother, for whom she has led the way
DAKAPAKI: (N.A. Ind.) a blossom
DALE: (Teut.) dweller in a vale between hills
DALLAS: (Teut.) playful; (Cymric) skilful
DALTA: (Gael.) a pet child
DAMA: (Hin.) temptress
DAMALIS: (Gr.) mild conqueror
DAMARIS: (Lat.) gentle
DAMASA: (Old Fr.) damsel
DAMIA: (Gr.) spirited
DANA: (Eng.) bright gift from God
DANAE: (Gr.) in mythology favourite of Jupiter and

mother of Perseus; golden shower

DANALA: (Eng.) golden; happy

DANELLA: (Teut.) wise mistress

DANETTE: (Heb.) God judges me; (Teut.) little mistress

DANICA: (Slav.) morning star

DANIELLE: (Heb.) judged by God; spiritual; feminine form of Daniel

DANILA: (Heb.) God judges

DAPHNE: (Gr.) sweet-smelling laurel or bay tree

DARA: (Heb.) compassionate

DARAKA: (Sans.) mild; timid

DARCIE: (Celt.) dark

DARDA: (Hung.) a dart; (Heb.) pearl of wisdom

DARE: (Gr.) defiance

DARIA: (Pers.) one who has knowledge

DARLENE: (Ang.-Sax.) variant of Darling

DASHA: (Rus.) darling

DAVINA: (Heb.) favourite, darling, beloved; feminine form of David

DAVITA: (Heb.) the beloved

DAWN: (Teut.) break of day

DEA: (Lat.) goddess

DEACON: (Gr.) joyful messenger

DEADORA: (Lat.-Gr.) gift of the goddess

DEBORAH: (Heb.) a bee, or queen bee; she rules

DECIMA: (Lat.) the tenth, or tenth girl in order of birth

DEIPHILA: (Gr.) divine love

DEIRDRE: (Celt.) sorrow or doubtful; (Irish) passionate

DELAMAY: (It.) of the spring

DELANEY: (Irish) enthusiastic

DELAROSA: (It.) of the rose

DELFINA: (Teut.) elfish

DELIA: (Gr.) of the island of Delos

DELICIA: (Lat.) delicately pleasant
DELIE: (Old Fr.) delicate, slender
DELILAH: (Heb.) alluring; temptress
DELINDA: (Teut.) gentle
DELIZEA: (It.) delight
DELLA: (Teut.) noble
DELMAR: (Teut.) dweller by the sea
DELORA: (Lat.) from the sea-coast
DELORES: (Span.) sorrowful woman
DELPHIA: (Gr.) pertaining to the Oracle of Delphi
DELPHINIA: (Gr.) loving sister
DELTA: (Gr.) the fourth; fourth letter of the Greek alphabet
DEMA: (Ang.-Sax.) an arbiter
DEMETER: (Gr.) fertile; goddess of the harvest
DEMI: (Fr.) half
DENA: (N.A. Ind.) a valley
DENANEER: (Arab.) piece of gold
DENISE: (Gr.) of Dionysius; feminine form of Denis
DERYN: (Wel.) small; birdlike
DESDEMONA: (Span.) literally, from a monkey; wife of Othello in Shakespeare's play of that name
DESIDERIA: (Lat.) desirable
DESIRATA: (Lat.) desired
DESIREE: (Lat.) desire; from 'desiderata', meaning desired
DESMA: (Gr.) child of a bond
DESMONDA: (Teut.) divinely protected
DESNA: (Hin.) giving
DESTINY: (Fr.) fated
DEVI: (Hin.) a goddess
DEVINA: (Lat.-Teut.) divine
DEVNET: (Celt.) white wave
DEVON: (Eng.) poetic
DEVONA: (Teut.) defensive; brave maid
DEVOTA: (Lat.) pious
DEXTRA: (Lat.) dexterous
DHARMA: (Hin.) morals, beliefs

DI: (Lat.) goddess; (Celt.) fire
DIADEMA: (Gr.) a diadem, badge of loyalty
DIAMANTA: (Lat.) of the diamond
DIANA: (Lat.) moon goddess
DIANEME: (Gr.) of divine origin
DIANTHE: (Gr.) divine flower; flower of the pink species
DIAPHENIA: (Gr.) transmitting light
DICA: (Slav.) cautious, careful
DICENTRA: (Gr.) flower name; known in old-fashioned gardens as bleeding heart
DIELLA: (Lat.) worshipper of God
DIERA: (Teut.) precious
DIGNA: (Lat.) worthy
DILLY: (Wel.) loyal
DINAH: (Heb.) from lawsuit: judged, avenged, vindicated
DINORAH: origin obscure; title of opera by Meyerbeer
DIONE: (Gr.) goddess of moisture
DIONETTE: (Gr.) little Dione
DISA: (Teut.) active spirit
DIVA: (Lat.) a goddess. In modern usage, a prima donna
DOBRANA: (Slav.) good
DOCILA, DOCILLA: (Lat.) flexible; willing to learn
DODI: (Gr.-Heb.) gift of God
DODO: (Heb.) loving
DOLFINE: (Teut.) noble wild one
DOLLY: English contraction of Dorothea
DOLORES: (Lat.) lady of sorrows; (Span.) Mary of the sorrows
DOMINA: (Lat.) mistress; lady of the household
DOMINICA: (Lat.) a child born on Sunday
DOMINIQUE: (Fr.) masterful; bright
DONABELLA: (Lat.) beautiful lady
DONALDA: (Celt.) little mistress

DONATA: (Lat.) a gift
DONELLA: (Lat.) little damsel
DONNA: (Span.) lady
DORA: (Gr.) a gift; also a diminutive of Dorothea and Dorothy
DORCAS: (Gr.) a gazelle
DORDIA: (Gr.-Heb.) gift from the Almighty
DOREA: (Gr.) a bounty; a gift
DOREEN: (Fr.) the gilded; probably an Irish form of Dorothy
DORENA: (Gr.) bountiful
DORENN: (Celt.) sullen
DORETTE: (Gr.) little gift
DORHISSA: (Heb.) gift of the oath
DORINA: (Heb.) perfection
DORINDA: (Gr.) given
DORIS: (Gr.) a sacrificial knife
DORITA: (Gr.) giver
DOROTHEA, DOROTHY: (Gr.) gift of God
DORY: (Fr.) gilded
DORYMENE: (Gr.) courageous
DOVA: (Teut.) dove, the emblem of peace and gentleness
DREDA: (Ang.-Sax.) thoughtful
DREW: (Gr.) a valorous woman
DROMICIA: (Gr.) swift
DRUSILLA: (Gr.) watered by the dew; (Lat.) strong
DUANA: (Celt.) a song
DULCINEA: (Lat.) sweet one
DULCY, DULCIE: English contractions of Dulcibella, from Latin 'dulcis' meaning sweet
DURETTA: (Span.) little steadfast one
DUSA: (Slav.) happy
DYANI: (N.A. Ind.) a deer
DYLAN: (Wel.) creative; from the sea
DYMPHNA: (Celt.) white wave
DYNA: (Gr.) power
DYOTA: (Sans.) light, sunshine
DYSIS: (Gr.) sunset

E

EANNA: (Irish) sunny
EARLA: (Eng.) leader
EARLENE: (Teut.) a noblewoman of high rank
EASTER: (Ang.-Sax.) young as the springtime
EBERTA: (Teut.) of bright mind
EBONY: (Gr.) dark and hard
EDA: (see Edith)
EDANA, EDENA, EDEVA: early forms of Edith
EDBURGA: (Ang.-Sax.) noble protection
EDEL: (Teut.) noble; clever
EDEN: (Heb.) paradise
EDGARDA: (Teut.) rich battle-maid
EDGINA: (Teut.-Gr.) born to wealth
EDIA: (Teut.) rich friend
EDINA: (Slav.) affluent
EDITH: (Ang.-Sax.) happy; (Teut.) rich gift. This name has been known in a Latinized form, 'Ediva'; also in England and other parts as Eda, Edie, Edithe
EDLA: (Teut.) a woman of noble family
EDLYN: (Teut.) rich gentlewoman
EDMEE: (Ang.-Sax.) fortunate protector
EDMONDA: (Teut.) happy protector; (Ang.-Sax.) the hand of happiness
EDNA: source unknown, but may have come from (Teut.) rich counsellor, or (Heb.) pleasure, perfect happiness
EDNAN: (Heb.) pleasure
EDRA: (Teut.) rich wisdom; (Heb.) woman of power
EDRIA: (Teut.) wealthy
EDWINA: a modern female form of Edwin
EEREENA: (Gr.) messenger of peace
EFFIE: a diminutive of Euphemia
EGBERTA: (Teut.) formidably bright
EGLANTYNE: (Eng.) plant name

EGLATINE: (Teut.) the sweet briar
EGLON: (Heb.) the gentle
EILEEN: (Gr.) a torch, a variant of Helen. Also spelt Aileen
EILIEN: (Gr.) light
EIRES: (Gr.) peaceful
ELA: (Nor.) holy
ELAIN, ELAINE: (Gr.) a torch; variants of Helen
ELAMA: (Gr.) from the high-land
ELANA: (Gr.) pretty
ELATA: (Lat.) exultant
ELBA: (Teut.) elfin wisdom
ELBERTA: (Teut.) nobly bright
ELDORA: (Teut.) gift of wisdom
ELDREDA, ELDRIDA: (Ang.-Sax.) wise friend
ELEANOR, ELEANORA, ELINOR: (Gr.) light; same as Helen, Helene
ELECTRA: (Gr.) yellow-haired
ELETA: (Span.) the astonished
ELFREDA, ELFRIDA: Old English compound of 'aelf' (elf) and 'thryth' (strength)
ELGA: (Ang.-Sax.) little fighter
ELGIVA: (Teut.) gift of the elves
ELIDA: (Lat.) the excluded
ELINEL: (Celt.) shapely
ELISABETH, ELIZABETH: (Heb.) God's oath; consecrated to God
ELISE: (Fr.) consecrated to God
ELISSA: (see Elizabeth)
ELITA: (Teut.) the chosen
ELLA: (Teut.) gift of the elf
ELLADORA: (Teut.) gift of the elves
ELLAMAE: (Teut.) elfin kinswoman
ELLEN: (Gr.) a torch; another form of Eleanor and Helen
ELLENIS: (Gr.) the original spelling of Helene, preceded by an aspirate
ELLIE: (see Eleanor, Ella)
ELLORA: (Gr.) happy
ELMA: (Gr.) love
ELODIE: (Gr.) fragile flower

ELOISA, ELOISE: (Teut.) celebrated holiness
ELOYS: (Teut.) famed holiness
ELPHIA: (Gr.) ivory
ELRICA: (Teut.) regal
ELSA: German derivative of Elisabeth. More commonly used after heroine in Wagner's opera *Lohengrin*
ELSIE: English diminutive of Elizabeth
ELSPETH: Scottish diminutive of Elizabeth
ELVA: (Teut.) elfin
ELVARETTA: (Teut.-Gr.) virtue
ELVERDA: (Gr.) the virgin
ELVETTA: (Teut.) wise little home-ruler
ELVIA: (Teut.) of keen mind
ELVINA: (Teut.) wise and friendly
ELVIRA: (Lat.) white; later popular in Spain
ELWY: (Wel.) benefit
ELWYN: (Wel.) white-browed
ELYSIA: (Lat.-Gr.) of paradise; divinely happy
EMANUELA: (Heb.) God is with thee
EMILIA: a variant of Emily
EMILY: derived from Emeline and Emmeline, meaning (Lat.-Teut.) industrious
EMINA: (Teut.) prominent
EMMA: (Teut.) signifying greatness. Old German form meaning whole or universal
EMOGENE: (Gr.) beloved child
EMRYS(S): (Celt.) immortal
ENA: modern usage, probably English form of Irish Eithne
ENDA: (Sans.) the last
ENFYS: (Wel.) rainbow
ENGRACIA: (Lat.) graceful
ENID: (Celt.) purity; (Wel.) lively
ENNIS: (Irish) dignified
ENONE: (Gr.) wayside flower
ENORE: (Eng.) careful
ERASMA: (Gr.) desired
ERDA: (Teut.) worldly
ERIANTHE: (Gr.)

sweetness of many flowers
ERICA: (Gr.) heather blossom; (Teut.) mighty heroine
ERIN: (Irish) based on Gaelic name for Ireland
ERINA: (Gael.) of Ireland; Irish girl
ERINNA: (Celt.) peace
ERLINA: (Ang.-Sax.) little elf
ERLINDA: (Span.) loyal
ERMA: (Teut.) noble maid
ERMENTRUD, ERMYNTRUDE: (Teut.) loyal maiden (of a nation)
ERMINIA: (Lat.) regal
ERNA: (Ang.-Sax.) retiring
ERNESTINE: earnestness; feminine form of Ernest
ESME: diminutive of Esmeralda
ESMERALDA: (Span.) emerald
ESSIE: (Pers.) star. Also diminutive of Esther
ESTELLE: (Fr.) shining star; form of Stella
ESTERA: (Pers.) star
ESTHER: generally supposed to come from the Persian word meaning star. The Old Testament gives it as Persian equivalent of the Hebrew 'Hadassah', myrtle
ESTRA: (Lat.) alien
ESTRELLA: (Span.) pertaining to star
ESWEN: (Wel.) strength
ETHEL: (Teut.) noble, or noble birth
ETHELIND: (Teut.) wise judge of people
ETHELINDA: (Ang.-Sax.) gracefully noble
ETHELREDA: (Teut.) noble counsellor
ETHELWYN: (Teut.) noble friend
ETTA: (Teut.) ruler of the home
EUCLEA: (Gr.) glorious
EUCLIDA: (Gr.) the calculating one
EUDOCIA: (Gr.) proven of high standard; well-taught by a wise father
EUDORA: (Gr.) happy gift

EUGENIA, EUGENIE: (Gr.) nobly born
EULALIA, EULALIE: (Gr.) of fair speech
EUNICE: (Gr.) happily victorious
EUPHEMIA, EUPHEMIE: (Gr.) speaker of words of good omen
EUPHRASIA, EUPHRASIE: (Gr.) joyful
EURWEN: (Wel.) golden-fair
EUSTACIA: (Gr.) fruitful
EVA: (see Eve)
EVADNE: (Gr.) fortunate
EVANGELINE: (Gr.) bringer of good news
EVANIA: (Gr.) obedient; (Irish) spirited
EVANTHE: (Gr.) lovely flower; she who is well decorated
EVE, EVIE: (Heb.) life; lively
EVELEEN: Irish diminutive of Eva
EVELYN: (Lat.) hazel nut; (Celt.) lively, pleasant; a variant of Eveleen
EVETTE: (Fr.) dainty
EVODIE: (Gr.) she who takes the right path
EXILDA: (Teut.) banished; (Lat.) the exiled
EZARA: (Heb.) little treasure

F

FABIA: (Lat.) Roman family name, signifying bean-grower
FABIOLA: (Lat.) woman of good works. Became popular in some religious families after publication in 1854 of book of same name, by Cardinal Wiseman
FABRIANNE: (Lat.) young woman of good works
FADIA: (Arab.) saved
FAE: (Old Fr.) she who trusts
FAIDA: (Arab.) bountiful
FAINE: (Ang.-Sax.) joyful
FAIRLIE: (Eng.) pet-name for Felicity
FAITH: (Teut.) unwavering

trust. Popular in Puritan times

FALDA: (Ice.) folded wings

FANIA: Slavonic form of Frances

FANNY: a diminutive of Frances

FANSHOM: (Teut.) free

FANTEEN: (Eng.) clever

FARAH: (Eng.) lovely

FARICA: (Teut.) peace-loving ruler

FATIMA: (Arab.) wise woman

FAUSTA, FAUSTINE: (Lat.) fortunate

FAVELA: (Span.) favoured

FAWN: (Fr.) young deer

FAWNIA: (Ang.-Sax.) joyous one

FAY, FAYE: (Old Fr.) fidelity, or faithful one; also fairy

FEDORA: (Gr.) gift of God

FELDA: (Teut.) inspired; (Ang.-Sax.) of the open country

FELICIA: variant of Felicity

FELICITY: (Lat.) happiness

FELIPA: (Gr.) lover of horses

FELITA: (Lat.) happy little one

FENELLA: (Celt.) white-shouldered

FENIA: (Scan.) gold worker

FERN: (Eng.) plant name

FERNON: (Teut.) distant

FERONIA: (Lat.) a goddess presiding over forests

FIDELIA: (Lat.) faithful one

FIDONIA: (Gr.) thrifty

FIFINELLA: (Fr.-It.) another form of Fifi, the French pet form of Josephine

FILIPA: (see Felipa)

FILMA: (Teut.) misty, hazy

FILOMENA: (Lat.) daughter of light

FINETTE: (Heb.) little addition

FINGAL: (Celt.) fair stranger

FINLEY: (Gael.) sunbeam

FINN: (Irish) cool

FINNA: (Celt.) white

FIONA: thought to have been invented by William Sharp for his literary character Fiona Macleod, or derived from Gaelic

'fionn' meaning fair, white
FIONNA: (Celt.) ivory-skinned
FLAVIA: (Lat.) blonde girl
FLAVILLA: (Lat.) yellow hair
FLETA: (Teut.) swift as an arrow; (Ang.-Sax.) fragrantly beautiful
FLEUR: (Fr.) flower
FLEURETTE: (Fr.) little flower
FLO: a contraction of Flora or Florence
FLORA: (Lat.) flowers; in mythology, goddess of flowers
FLORANTHE: (Lat.-Gr.) flower-blossom
FLORENCE: (Lat.) blooming; flourishing
FLORETTA, FLORETTE: (Lat.) little flower
FLORIAN: (Lat.) flowery
FLORIMEL: (Lat.-Gr.) honey-flower
FLORINDA: Spanish form of Flora
FLORIS: (Lat.) a flower
FLUR: (Celt.) a flower
FONDA: (Lat.) deep, profound woman
FORTUNA: (Lat.) goddess of fortune; lucky
FOSSETTA: (Fr.) dimpled
FRANCES: (Teut.) free
FRANCESCA: (It.) form of Frances – free
FRANCIS: (Fr.) French or Frankish
FREA: (Scan.) lady
FREDA: a diminutive of Winifred
FREDELLA: (Teut.) peaceful elf
FREDERICA: (Teut.) peaceful ruler; feminine form of Frederick
FREDICIA: (Teut.) peace-ruler
FREDLINA: (Teut.) wise and peaceful
FRESA: (Teut.) curly-haired
FREYA: (Scan.) a lady of love; Norse goddess of love and beauty
FRIDESWIDE: (Ang.-Sax.) peaceably strong
FRITZIE: (Teut.) peaceful ruler

FRODINE: (Teut.) wise friend
FROMA: (Teut.) holy
FRONIA: (Gr.) a thinker
FULCA: (Lat.) accomplished, capable

G

GABRIELLE: (Heb.) heroine of God
GADA: (Heb.) fortune
GAERWEN: (Wel.) a place name; literally white fort
GAIA: (Gr.) earth goddess
GAIL: a contraction of Abigail
GALATEA: (Gr.) milk-white. In Greek mythology, a sea nymph who loved Acis
GALATIA: (Gr.) laughing girl
GALE: (Ang.-Sax.) pleasant, happy; a pet form of Abigail
GALIENA: (Rus.) steady
GALINA: (Rus.) deserving
GAMBLE: (Scan.) old
GARDA: (Teut.) prepared
GARDENIA: (Eng.) after the flower-name
GARIMA: (Hin.) warm
GARLANDA: (Lat.) adorned with flowers
GARNET: (Lat.) like the precious gem; (Teut.) a jewel (also a male name)
GASPARINE: (Pers.) a horse-woman
GAVIOTA: (Span.) sea-gull
GAVRA: (Heb.) God is my rock
GAY: probably a diminutive of the French, Gayla; or direct from the adjective
GAYLA: (Fr.) the joyous one (from Gal); (Teut.) merry
GAYNA: probably a form of Guinevere
GAZA: (Gr.) earth
GEBRA: (Gr.) graceful
GELASIA: (Gr.) laughing girl
GEMINI: (Gr.) born in May; twin
GEMMA: (Lat.) a gem
GENERA: (Gr.) high-born
GENESIA: (Lat.) newcomer
GENEVA: (Teut.) a distilled spirit

GENEVIEVE: (Celt.) white wave
GENEVRA: an English contraction of Genevieve
GENNA: (Eng.) womanly
GENOA: (It.) playful
GEORGETTE: a French derivative of George
GEORGIA: feminine form of George (Lat.) farmer
GEORGINA: (Gr.) husband-woman; derivative of George
GERALDA: (Teut.) courageous
GERALDINE: (Teut.) fair battle-maid; feminine form of Gerald
GERDA: (Teut.) girdled
GERMAINE: (Teut.) akin, belonging
GERTRUDE: (Teut.) spear maid
GERVAISE: (Fr.) strong
GHITA: (It.) pearl
GIACINTA: (Gr.) dark flower
GIANINA: (Heb.) the Lord's grace
GIANNA: (It.) forgiving
GIGI: (Fr.) small
GILA: (Heb.) joyful
GILBERTA: (Teut.) bright pledge
GILDA: (Ang.-Sax.) golden; (Celt.) God's servant
GILLIAN: English form of Julia
GILMORY: (Celt.) Mary's servant
GINA: (Jap.) silvery
GINGER: (Lat.) pet form of Virginia – a maid, virgin
GIRALDA: (Teut.) powerful contender; Italian form of Geraldine
GISALA, GISELA: (Teut.) a pledge
GISELLE: (Teut.) a hostage
GITA: (Sans.) song
GITHA: (Ang.-Sax.) war
GITTA: (Heb.) goodness
GITTLE: (Heb.) innocent flatterer
GLADYS: Welsh form of Claudia. Also Gwladys
GLEDA: (Ice.) make glad
GLENDA: (Wel.) holy
GLENDORA: (Teut.-Gr.) gift of the glen
GLENICE, GLENYSS:

(Gael.) from the mountain glen
GLENIS, GLENYS: (Wel.) good, pure
GLENNA: (Gael.) a valley maiden
GLINDA: origin unknown; probably a variant of Glenda
GLINYS: (Wel.) little valley
GLORIA: (Lat.) glory
GLORIANA: (Lat.-Heb.) glorious grace
GLYNIS: (see Glinys)
GODEBERTA: (Teut.) divine brightness; (Lat.) a girl who serves God
GODELEVA: (Lat.) a girl of God's brightness
GODINE: (Teut.) God's friend
GODIVA: (Teut.) divine gift. 'Godgifu' (Latinized as Godiva) was a heroine of the eleventh-century Coventry legend
GOEWIN, GOEWYN: (Wel.) sprightly
GONDOLINE: (Teut.) wise, brave one
GONERIL: (Lat.) honoured
GRACE, GRACIE: (Lat.) elegance, or beauty of form and movement
GRACIA, GRATIA: (Lat.) favour, grace; the graceful one
GRACIENNE: (Lat.) little one
GRACIOSA: (Span.) gracefully attractive
GRAINE: (Celt.) love
GRANIA: (Celt.) affectionate love
GRATIANA: the grateful Anne
GRAZINA: (It.) grace, favour, charm
GREDEL: (Teut.) the pearl
GREER: (Gr.) the watchwoman
GREGORIA: (Gr.) the watcher
GRETA: Swedish abbreviation of Margaret
GRETCHEN: (Pers.) pearl; a German contraction of Margaret
GRETEL: a variant of Gredel
GRIMONIA: (Lat.) venerable woman
GRISELDA: (Teut.)

indomitable maid; some authorities give it as stone of heroism
GRISELDIS: (Teut.) grey battle-maid
GRIZEL, GRISELL: variants of Griseldis
GROVENA: (Teut.) dweller of the grove
GRYTA: (Lit.) good
GUDILA: (Teut.) God helps
GUDRID: (Teut.) divine impulse
GUDRUN: (Scan.) wise
GUDULA: (Lat.) good daughter
GUIDA: (Celt.) sensible; (Teut.) a guide
GUINEVERE: (Wel.-Ang.-Sax.) the fair wife; (Celt.) white wave
GULLA: (Scan.) yellow
GUNDRED: (Teut.) wise and brave
GUNHILD, GUNHILDA: (Teut.) battle-maid in war
GUNI: (Teut.) divine freshness
GWEN, GWENDA: abbreviations of Gwendolen
GWENDOLEN: (Celt.) white-bow
GWENDYDD: (Wel.) star of morning
GWENEAL: (Celt.) white angel
GWENNOL: (Wel.) the swallow
GWENOG: (Wel.) smiling
GWLITHYN: (Wel.) dew-drop
GWYLFAI: (Wel.) festival of May
GWYNETH: (Celt.) blessed
GWYNNE: (Celt.) white
GYDA: (Teut.) gift
GYNETH: (Celt.) fair one
GYPSY: (Eng.) adventurer
GYPSY: wanderer; origin not definite, but probably Indian
GYTHA: (Ang.-Sax.) war

H

HABIKA: (Arab.) cherished one
HADRIA: (Lat.) of the Adriatic

HAFWEN: (Wel.) beauty of summer
HAGAR: (Heb.) timid stranger; flight
HAGGAI: (Heb.) one who is festive
HAGIR: (Arab.) wanderer
HAIDEE: (Gr.) modest
HAILEY, HAYLEY: (Eng.) natural
HAIMA: (Sans.) made of gold
HALCYON: (Lat.-Gr.) calm, peaceful. Thought to have come from 'halsion', a kingfisher which nested on a calm sea
HALDIS: (Teut.) spirit of the stone; firm
HALEA: (Haw.) halo
HALENA: (Slav.-Gr.) light
HALETTE: (Ang.-Sax.) tiny queen
HALIMA: (Arab.) gentle
HALIMEDA: (Gr.) sea-moss
HALINA: (Rus.) faithful
HALLE: (Teut.) ruler of the home
HALONA: (N.A. Ind.) happy, fortunate times
HAMELINE: (Teut.) fond of home
HANA: (Jap.) flower; (Arab.) delight
HANNAH: (Heb.) favoured of God
HANUSIA: (Heb.) grace of the Lord
HARD: (Jap.) spring
HARELDA: (Scan.) sea duck
HARMONIA: (Gr.) unity
HARRIET: (Teut.) mistress of the home
HASITA: (Sans.) laughing
HATTIE, HATTY: diminutive forms of Harriet
HAVA: (Heb.) lively
HAZEL: (Teut.) brown; (Heb.) protected by God
HEATHER: (Teut.) a beautiful flowering shrub. A favourite Scottish name
HEBE: (Gr.) personification of youth. In mythology, goddess of youth; cupbearer to the gods
HEDDA: (Teut.) a haven in trouble; derived from Hedwig

HEDIA: (Gr.) pleasing
HEDONA: (Gr.) extreme delight
HEDVA: (Gr.) industrious worker
HEDWIG: (Teut.) haven in trouble
HEDY: (Teut.) a pet form of Hedwig
HEIDI: Swiss name based on Adelheid (Adelaide)
HELBONA: (Heb.) fruitful
HELEN, HELENA: (Gr.) light
HELGA: (Gr.) holy
HELIANTHE: (Gr.) bright flower; sunflower
HELIE: (Gr.) sunny
HELISE: (Gr.) of the Elysian fields
HELMA: (Ang.-Sax.) a helm or rudder; (Teut.) helmet
HELOISE: (Teut.) some references give it as famous warrior; others a variant of Helewidis from 'haila', sound, and 'vid', wide
HELONIA: (Gr.) a marsh lily
HELSA: (Heb.) given to God
HELVITIA: (Lat.) high hill dwelling
HENDRIKA: (Teut.) ruler of the home
HENRIETTA, HENRIETTE: (Teut.) ruler of the home. Also feminine form of Henry
HEPHZIBAH: (Heb.) my delight is in her. Name of wife of Hezekiah
HERA: (Gr.) heroine; protector of women. In Greek mythology Hera (or Here) goddess of marriage
HERLIZA: (Span.) sweet
HERMA: (Teut.) beloved
HERMANDINE: (Teut.) a warrior's sweetheart
HERMIA: (Gr.) stately
HERMILLA: (Span.) fighter
HERMIONE: (Lat.) kindred; maid of high degree
HERO: (Gr.) in mythology beloved of Leander, for whom he swam the Hellespont; sometimes given as mistress of the house

HERRA: (Gr.) girl of the earth
HERTHA: (Teut.) goddess of fertility
HESNA: (Arab.) star
HESPER: (Gr.) night star
HESTER, HESTHER: (see Esther)
HESTIA: (Gr.) in mythology, goddess of the hearth
HETTY: English diminutive of Harriet
HEULWEN: (Wel.) sunshine
HIBERNIA: (Lat.) Ireland
HILA: (Heb.) angelic
HILARY: (Lat.) cheerful, merry
HILDA: (Teut.) battle-maid
HILDEBRAND: (Teut.) strong
HILDEGARDE: (Teut.) protecting battle-maid
HILINA: (Haw.) celestial
HINDA: (Heb.) held high
HIROKO: (Jap.) wise; giving
HOHOKA: (N.A. Ind.) wild dove
HOKU: (Haw.) star-like
HOLLY: (Ang.-Sax.) holy; English plant-name associated with Christmas
HONESTA: (Lat.) honourable
HONEY: (Lat.) sweet-hearted
HONOR, HONORA, HONORIA: (Lat.) reputation; sense of what is right and true
HOPE: (Ang.-Sax.) trust; expectation of good
HORATIA: (Lat.) careful; time-keeper
HORTENSE, HORTENSIA: (Lat.) at home in a garden
HOSANNA: (Gr.) worshipful
HOSEA: (Heb.) salvation
HOWIN: (Chin.) a loyal swallow
HUBERTA: (Teut.) bright in spirit; feminine form of Hubert
HUELINE: (Teut.) clever
HUGA: (Teut.) intellectual
HUGUETTE: (Teut.) feminine form of Hugh – thoughtful, intellectual

HULDA: (Nor.) muffled; covered
HULDAH: (Heb.) weasel
HULLE: (Dutch) veiled
HYACINTH: (Gr.) flower of the royal purple; (Lat.) sapphire
HYPATIA: (Gr.) superior

I

IANESSA: (Gr.) gentle ruler
IANTHE: (Gr.) the violet, symbol of modesty
IANTHINE: (Gr.) like the violet
IBETH: (Span.) God's promise; variant form of Elizabeth
IBSEN: (Scan.) scholarly
ICASIA: (Teut.) god-like; (Gr.) happy
IDA: (Gr.) happy
IDAHLIA: (Gr.) sweet
IDALAH: (Heb.) one who proceeds softly or snares
IDALIA: (Gr.) happiness
IDALINE: (Gr.) the far-seeing
IDE: (Irish) thirsty
IDELIA: (Teut.) noble
IDELLE: (Gr.-Teut.) clever, happy one; (Celt.) generous
IDETTE: (Gr.) happy little one
IDIL: (Lat.) pleasant
IDINA: (Scan.) work
IDLE: (Gr.) cloud at dawn
IDMONIA: (Gr.) skilful
IDOLA: (Lat.) idolized
IDONA: (Scan.) fresh
IDONEA: (Lat.) proper; (Scan.) Norse spring goddess
IDONETTE: (Lat.) proper little lady who never works
IDONY: (Scan.) reborn
IESHA: (Arab.) feminine
IGNATIA, IGNACIA: (Lat.) the fiery or ardent one
IGNES: (Lat.) pure
IKEA: (Scan.) smooth
IKU: (Jap.) nurturing
ILA: (Ang.-Sax.) insulate; island-dweller
ILANA: (Heb.) gorgeous
ILDE: (Teut.) battle-maid
ILENA: (Gr.) regal

ILKA: (Gael.) every; (Hung.) beauty
ILONE: (Hung.) radiant beauty; (Gr.) light
ILONKA: (Slav.) lovely
ILSA: (Gael.) glowing
ILYTHIA: (Gr.) goddess presiding over childbirth
IMALA: (N.A. Ind.) strong-willed
IMANA, IMANI: (Arab.) faithful
IMELDA: (Old Eng.) the moderate one
IMOGEN: (Gr.) beloved child
IMOGENA, IMOGENE: (Lat.) visionary, an image; (Gr.) beloved child
IMPERIA: (Lat.) imperious
INA: (Lat.) small
INAS: (Arab.) friendly
INCA: (Teut.) dweller in the meadow
INDIGO: (Lat.) blue-eyed
INDIRA: (Hin.) powerful; the god of thunder
INES: (Gr.) a daughter; (Span.) pure, chaste
INESSA: (Rus.) pure
INEX: (Gr.) pure; Portuguese form of Agnes
INEZ: (Gr.) pure
INGEBORG: (Teut.) tower of protection
INGRID: (Nor.) maiden of the Ingvaeones
INKA: (Scan.) abundant
INNOCENTIA: (Lat.) unknowing of evil
IOLA: (Gr.) dawn
IONA: (Gr.) violet jewel; Greek flower-name
IORWEN: (Wel.) lord; beautiful
IPHIGENIA: (Gr.) of a royal and courageous race
IRA: (Heb.) contended; watchful
IRENE: (Gr.) peace; messenger of peace
IRETTE: (Teut.) little wrathful one
IRIAN: (Gr.) rare
IRIS: (Gr.) the rainbow; (Lat.) goddess of the rainbow
IRMA: (Teut.) maid of high degree

IRMADEL: (Teut.) noble maiden
IRMALEE: (Teut.) Irma of the meadow
IRMIN: (Lat.) regal; a variant of ermine, the royal fur
IRRA: (Gr.) serene
ISA: (Teut.) with a spirit like iron
ISABEL, ISABELLA, ISABELLE: variant forms of Elizabeth
ISADORA: (Gr.) a gift
ISAURA: (Gr.) soft air
ISCAR: (Heb.) she who watches
ISEULT: (Celt.) fair
ISHA: (Hin.) protected
ISLA: (Old Fr.) island; (Lat.) insular
ISLAMEY: (Arab.) obedient to the will of Allah
ISLEAN: (Celt.) of sweet voice
ISMENA: (Gr.) learned one
ISOLA: (Lat.) alone; set apart
ISOLDE: (see Iseult)
ISOTTA: (Celt.) the fair
ITA: (Celt.) thirsty one
ITICA: (Span.) eloquent
IVA: (Rus.) willow; (Slav.) dedicated
IVANNA: (Rus.) gift from God
IVENA: (Heb.) grace of the Lord
IVORY: (Lat.) white
IVY: (Teut.) a clinging vine; constancy
IXIA: (Gr.) the mistletoe
IZORA: (Arab.) dawn

J

JACEY: (Gr.) sparkling
JACINT(H)A: (Gr.) wearer of the purple
JACINTH: name of precious stone, probably from (Gr.) hyacinth
JACQUELINE: (Heb.) the supplanter
JACQUETTE: (Heb.) the little supplanter
JADA: (Span.) precious; personable
JADE: (Span.) courageous; gemstone
JADEN: (Heb.) God has heard

JAE: (Lat.) small; jay bird
JAELA: (Heb.) bright
JAHOLA: (Heb.) a dove
JAIME: (Fr.) loving girl
JAKIRA: (Arab.) warmth
JALILA: (Arab.) excellent
JAMIE: (Heb.) fun-loving
JANAN: (Arab.) soulful
JANE: (Heb.) grace of God; feminine form of John
JANEL: (Fr.) fun-loving, exuberant
JANET: (Heb.) little one of divine grace
JANICE: (Heb.) knowing the grace of God
JANNAH: (Heb.) the Lord graciously gave
JANSEN: (Scan.) smooth
JARITA: (Hin.) motherly devotion
JARVIA: (Old Eng.) feminine form of Jarvis – a driver
JASIA: (Slav.) hopeful
JASMINE: (Pers.) from Yasmin; flower name
JAVOTTE: (Celt.) white stream or wave
JAYA: (Hin.) winning
JEAN: Scottish form of Jane, Joan or Johanna
JEANNETTE: a variant of Jean, which is a Scottish form of Jane (Heb.) meaning grace of God
JECA: (Slav.) untainted
JELENA: (Gr.) light
JEMIMA: (Arab.) the doer; (Heb.) a dove
JENA: (Arab.) small
JENIKA: (Eng.) blonde
JENNA: (Eng.) gracious; form of Jean
JENNIFER: (Celt.) white phantom or white wave
JENNY: pet-name for Jane and Jennifer
JENO: (Gr.) heavenly
JENOVA: (It.) playful
JERUSHA: (Heb.) the exiled; some references give this as possession
JESKA: (Heb.) she who looks out
JESSICA: (Heb.) He beholds, or God's grace
JESSIE: form of Janet, chiefly Scottish
JESSLYN, JESSELINE: (Heb.) wealthy woman
JEVAE: (Span.) one who is desired

JEVERA: (Heb.) life
JEWEL: (Old Fr.) joy
JILL: pet form of Gillian and Julia
JINTE: (Hin.) patient
JOAN: (see Jane)
JOANNA, JOHANNA: (Heb.) grace of the Lord
JOCELIN, JOCELYN: (Lat.) playful
JOCUNDA: (Lat.) mirthful
JODETTE: (Lat.) sportive one
JODIS: (Teut.) horse sprite
JOFRID: (Teut.) lover of horses
JOLANTA: (Gr.) lovely girl
JOLETTA: (Lat.) the violet, symbol of modesty
JOLINE: (Eng.) blessed
JONEA: (Heb.) the Lord's grace
JONITA: (Heb.) pretty little one
JORDANA: (Heb.) descendant
JORNA: (Span.) one who journeys
JOSCELIND: (Lat.) gentle playmate
JOSEPHINE: French feminine derivative of Joseph
JOVITA: (Lat.) merry; derived from Jove (Jupiter)
JOY: (Teut.) pleasure; (Lat.) gladness, a jewel
JOYAN: (Old Fr.) rejoicing
JOYCE: (Teut.) to enjoy; (Lat.) merry; a Celtic saint
JOYLEEN: modern usage
JOYVITA: (Lat.) jovial
JUANITA: Spanish form of Jane
JUDE: (Fr.) confident
JUDITH: (Heb.) praised of the Lord; a Jewess
JUDY: English contraction of Judith
JULIA: (Lat.) downy-face; feminine form of Julius
JULIANA: Spanish form of Julia
JULIET, JULIETTE: other forms of Julia, Shakespeare took it from Italian Giuliette, from Giulia, or Julia
JUN: (Chin.) truth; (Jap.) obedient

JUNE: (Lat.) ever faithful; from the goddess Juno
JUNIATA: (Lat.) ever youthful
JUNILLA: (Lat.) little maid who is ever youthful
JUNO: heavenly; in Roman mythology the wife of Jupiter
JUSTICIA: (Lat.) the just
JUSTINE: (Lat.) the righteous one
JUVENTIA: (Lat.) goddess of youth

K

KACEY: (Irish) daring
KACHINA: (N.A. Ind.) sacred dance
KADENZA: (Lat.) cadence; one who dances
KAELA, KALEA: (Arab.) sweet
KAI: (Haw.) the sea
KAILAH: (Gr.) virtuous
KAITLIN: (Irish) pure of heart
KALA: (Hin.) royal; black
KALAMA: (N.A. Ind.) the wild goose
KALDORA: (Gr.) beautiful gift
KALEY: (Sans.) energetic
KALI: (Gr.) beauty
KALMA: (Teut.) calm
KALONICA: (Gr.) the victory of beauty
KALWA: (Finn.) heroic
KALYA: (Sans.) healthy
KALYANA: (Sans.) one who is virtuous
KALYCA: (Gr.) rosebud
KAMA: (Sans.) desired
KAMAMA: (N.A. Ind.) butterfly
KAMEA: (Haw.) beloved, adored
KANE: (Jap.) golden
KANYA: (Hin.) virginal
KARA: (Dan.) beloved friend; form of Cara
KARABEL: (Span.) beautiful face
KAREN: Danish form of Katherine
KARENA: (Gr.) pure
KARIMA: (Arab.) giving
KARINA: (Gr.) a variation of Katherine, pure

KARINE: (Rus.) pure
KARISSA: (Gr.) long-suffering
KARLA: (Teut.) much-loved
KARMA: (Sans.) destiny
KARMIT: (N.A. Ind.) nature
KASAMIRA: (Slav.) peace-maker
KASIA: (Gr.) pure
KATANIYA: (Heb.) little girl
KATE, KATIE: contractions of Katherine
KATHARINE, KATHERINE: (Gr.) pure, name of virgin martyr of Alexandria
KATHINI: (Kikuyu) little bird
KATHLEEN: (Celt.) beautiful eyes; also Irish form of Katherine
KATHRYN, KATRINE: variant forms of Katherine
KATIA: (Fr.) fashionable, stylish
KATINKA: Russian form of Katherine
KAULIKA: (Sans.) nobly born
KAY: (Gr.) I rejoice
KAYA: (N.A. Ind.) little elder sister
KAYLA: (Gr.) pure
KEELEY: (Irish) noisy
KEENA: (Irish) brave
KEIKO: (Haw.) child of joy
KEILA: (Heb.) crowned
KEIRA: (Gael.) dark
KELDA: (Scan.) a spring or fountain
KELLY: (Irish) brave
KENDRA: (Ang.-Sax.) a woman of knowledge; (Teut.) understanding
KERRY: (provincial English) a large apron
KESHENA: (N.A. Ind.) swift in flight
KETURAH: (Heb.) fragrance
KEVALA: (Sans.) one's own
KEYNE: (Celt.) jewel
KEZIAH: (Heb.) the cassia tree
KHALINDA: (Hin.) eternal
KIARA: (It.) illustrious
KIKO: (Jap.) lively
KIMBERLEY: (Eng.) leader

KIMI: (Jap.) spiritual
KIN: (Jap.) golden
KINA: (Gr.) Christian messenger
KINETA: (Gr.) active
KIRA: (Rus.) light-hearted
KIRBY: (Ang.-Sax.) one from the church-town
KIRSTY: (Gr.) Christian. Scottish contraction of Christina
KITTY: a contraction of Katherine
KLARA: (Hung.) bright
KLEANTHA: (Gr.) celebrated flower
KLYMENA: (Gr.) celebrated
KOA: (Heb.) princess
KOLFINNA: (Celt.) cool, white lady
KOLINA: (Gr.) pure
KOLOTOSA: (N.A. Ind.) star
KOMALA: (Sans.) charming
KORA: (Gr.) practical
KOREN: (Gr.) a maiden
KORINA: (Gr.) maiden
KOTSASI: (N.A. Ind.) white flower
KUKI: (Jap.) snow
KUNI: (Jap.) country born
KWAI: (Chin.) fragrance of a rose
KWONG: (Chin.) broad
KYLA: (Gael.) comely
KYLIE: (Irish) graceful
KYNA: (Gr.) lady
KYRA: (Gr.) feminine

L

LABANA: (Heb.) ivory goddess
LABITTA: (Lat.) the girl with the luscious lips; from labium, the lip
LACEY: (Gr.) cheerful
LACRETIA: (Lat.) efficient
LADORNA: (Lat.) embellished
LAINA: (Teut.) denial
LAKELA: (Haw.) feminine
LAKESHA: (Eng.) favoured
LALA: (Slav.) the tulip
LALAGE: (Gr.) a prattler, talkative one
LALITA: (Sans.) the pleasing, cherished one
LALLA: (Scottish) of the lowlands; used by

Thomas Moore for his poem, 'Lalla Rookh' (1817)

LALYA: (Lat.) eloquent

LAMIA: (Egyp.) calm

LANA: (Lat.) the soft, woolly one; short form of Alana (Celt.) my child

LANAI: (Haw.) heavenly

LANITIA: (Slav.) unique

LARA: (Lat.) famous

LARAINE: (Lat.) pretty

LARENTIA: (Lat.) foster-mother

LARINA: (Lat.) sea-gull; (Gr.) the plump one

LARISSA: (Lat.) the bright and shining one; in ancient Greece the chief town of Thessaly

LARSEN: (Scan.) crowned with laurels

LASHA: (Span.) forlorn

LATONIA, LATONIE: (Lat.-Gr.) mother of Apollo; sometimes given as mother of the sun

LATRICE: (Lat.) noble

LAUDA: (Lat.) praise

LAUDETTE: (Lat.) little praiseworthy one

LAURA: (Lat.) the laurel. Latin form of Laurence

LAUREN: (Lat.) crowned with laurels

LAURENT: (Fr.) graceful

LAURETTE: (Lat.) little victorious one

LAURIE: (Eng.) careful

LAURINDA: a variant of Laura

LAVEDA: (Lat.) pure

LAVENA: (Celt.) joy

LAVENDER: (Lat.) flower name; peaceful

LAVERNE: (Fr.) like the spring

LAVINIA: (Lat.) the cleansed. Name of daughter of Latinus, the second wife of Aeneas

LAYLA: (Arab.) dark

LEAH: (Lat.) weary; (Heb.) cow

LEAL: (Celt.) faithful

LEALA: (Fr.) steadfast

LEANNA, LEANNE: combination of Lee and Anna

LEANORA: (Gr.) light

LEATRICE: (Lat.) young and joyful

LEDA: (Heb.) beautiful temptress. In Greek mythology mother of Helen and Clytemnestra

LEE: (Chin.) plum

LEENA: (Lat.) temptress

LEFA: (Teut.) the heart of a plant or tree

LEIGH: (Eng.) light-footed

LEILA: (Arab.-Pers.) dark, or dark oriental beauty

LEILANI: (Haw.) heavenly flower

LELIA: (Teut.) loyal

LEMMUELA, LEMUELA: (Heb.) devoted to God

LENA: a diminutive of Helen(a)

LENICE: (Gr.) feminine form of Leonard – brave as a lion

LENITA: (Lat.) gentle spirit

LENKA: (Slav.) light

LENT: a German diminutive of Magdalene

LENTULA: (Celt.) mild

LEODA: (Teut.) woman of the people

LEOLA: (Lat.) fierce

LEOLIE: (N.A. Ind.) prairie flower

LEONA: (Lat.-Fr.) feminine form of Leo – strong and brave as a lion

LEONIE: French form of Leon; feminine form of Leo

LEONORA: (Gr.) light. Leonora the Italian, Leonore the French, Lenore the German forms

LEONTI(Y)NE: (Lat.) like a lioness

LEOPOLDINE: (Teut.) of bold people

LEORA: (Gr.) lighthearted

LERA: (Rus.) strong

LESBIA: (Gr.) a woman of the island of Lesbos

LESLEY: feminine form of Leslie

LETA: (Lat.) joyful

LETTICE, LAETITIA: (Lat.) gladness, joy

LETTY: a variant of Lettice

LEVANA: (Heb.) fair

LEVINA: (Lat.) lightning

LEWANNA: (Heb.) the moon

LEWINA: (Heb.) little battle-prize

LEXI, LEXIE: (Gr.) sparkling
LEYLA: (Arab.) night
LIAN: (Chin.) graceful willow
LIANA: (Lat.) a plant-name
LIBBY: an English contraction of Elizabeth
LIBERTY: (Lat.) free
LIBNA: (Heb.) fair
LIDA: (Slav.) people's love
LIESEL: (Teut.) pretty
LILA: (Pers.) lilac
LILIAN, LILIAS: (Lat.) lily; purity
LILITH: (Heb.) a serpent, the Assyrian goddess of night
LILY: (Lat.) the bloom; (Gr.) symbol of purity
LILYBELLE: a combination of Lily and Belle; beautiful lily
LINDA: (Lat.) handsome; a contraction of Belinda
LINDALOU: combination of Linda and Louise – war heroine
LINDSAY: (Eng.) bright, shining
LINETTE: (Fr.-Eng.) graceful
LING: (Ch.) delicate
LINNEA: (Scan.) linden tree
LINNET: (Celt.) shapely
LINTRUDE: (Teut.) of serpent strength
LIORA: (Heb.) light
LIRA: (Gr.) lyre
LIRIA: (Gr.) delicate
LISA, LISE, LIZA, LIZZIE: contractions of Elizabeth
LISBET: (Scan.) sweet
LISLE: (Fr.) the island
LITA: diminutive of any name ending in lita
LIVIA: diminutive of Olivia, the olive tree, symbol of peace
LLAWELA: (Wel.) feminine form of Llewellyn – leader, lightning
LLINOS: (Wel.) the linnet
LOGAN: (Eng.) climbing
LOIETU: (N.A. Ind.) a flower; farewell to spring
LOIS: (Gr.) desirable, good
LOLA: (Teut.) virile; a Spanish diminutive of Dolores
LOLETA: (Span.) maid of the sorrows

LOLITA: (Span.) sad
LORA: (Lat.) regal
LORI: (Flem.) the lazy one
LORINDA: (Lat.) the learned; another form of Laura
LORIS: (Lat.) slow
LORNA: a feminine form of Lorn(e); from the Ang.-Sax, lost
LORRAINE: (Fr.) derived from the province of Lorraine
LOTTIE, LOTTY: English diminutives of Charlotte
LOTUS: (Egyp.) flower of forgetting
LOUELLA: (Teut.) shrewd war heroine
LOUISA, LOUISE: (Teut.) war heroine; feminine variants of Louis
LOURDES: (Fr.) hallowed; girl from Lourdes
LUBA: (Ang.-Sax.-Slav.) my beloved
LUBRA: (Slav.) lover
LUCIA: (Lat.) light, daybreak
LUCIANNA: (Lat.) gracious gift
LUCIDA: (Lat.) shining
LUCILLE: (Lat.) light-shedding
LUCINDA: (Lat.) shining, clear
LUCIOLA: (Lat.) a firefly
LUCIPPE: (Gr.) white horse
LUCRECE, LUCRETIA: (Lat.) born at dawn
LUCY: (Lat.) born at daybreak; feminine form of Lucius
LUDMILLA: (Slav.) loved by the people
LUDWINIA: (Teut.) the people's friend
LULETTE: (Teut.) little comforter
LULITA: (Sans.) agitated
LULU: (N.A. Ind.) a rabbit; (Pers.) a jewel
LUMAI: (N.A. Ind.) the humming of birds' wings
LUNA: (Lat.) shining; goddess of the half-moon
LUNEDA: (Celt.) shapely
LUNETTA: (Lat.) little moon
LUPE: (Lat.) the wolfess; (Teut.) prophecy of good fortune

LYDIA: (Gr.) a maid of Lydia
LYNETTE: (see Linnet)
LYNN: (Gr.) a refreshing water pool
LYNNA: (Teut.) a cascade
LYRIS: (Gr.) song of the lyre
LYSANDRA: (Gr.) liberator

M

MABEL: (Celt.) mirth; the English form of Amabel
MABEN: (Wel.) child
MABYN: (Wel.) youthful
MACARIA: (Span.) blessed
MACEY: (Fr.) Matthew's estate
MACKENZIE: (Irish) leader
MADDISON, MADISON: (Eng.) child of the great warrior
MADDOX: (Eng.) giving
MADELINE, MAGDALEN: (Heb.) woman of Magdala; name much used after supposed discovery of relics of St Mary Magdalene in thirteenth century
MADGE: English contraction of Margaret
MADHURA: (Sans.) charming
MADONNA: (Lat.) my lady
MADORA: (Gr.) my gift
MADRA: (Lat.) mother
MAE: (Ang.-Sax.) kinswoman
MAEVE: (Irish) queen
MAGASKI: (N.A. Ind.) white swan
MAGDA: form of Magdalene and Magdaline (see Magdala)
MAGDALA: (Gr.) a tower; (Heb.) woman of Magdala
MAGDALENE: (see Madeline)
MAGGIE: Scottish form of Margaret
MAGINA: (Rus.) hard-working
MAGNOLIA: an allusion to the tree and flower of that name, so called in honour of Pierre Magnol, French botanist

MAHALA: (Heb.) sweet singer; (N.A. Ind.) woman
MAHINA: (Haw.) moonbeam
MAHIRA: (Heb.) vibrant
MAHLAH: (Heb.) melodious song
MAHOLA: (Heb.) dancer
MAHSA: (Arab.) a little moon
MAIA: (Gr.) earth goddess; fertile
MAIDA: (Teut.) maiden; place name in Italy
MAIRE: Irish form of Mary
MAISHA: (Arab.) proud
MAISIE: Scottish diminutive of Margaret
MAJULA: (Slav.) star
MAKAYLA: a variant form of Michaela
MALAK: (Arab.) angelic
MALCA: (Teut.) industrious
MALIKA: (Hung.) hardworking; punctual
MALINDA: (Gr.) honey; (Old Eng.) gentle
MALITA: (N.A. Ind.) salmon
MALLORY: (Fr.) tough
MALTA: (Pho.) refuge
MALVA: (Gr.) the soft one; (Lat.) plant-name
MALVINA: (Gael.) from 'maol-mhin' meaning smooth brow
MAMIE: an American diminutive of Mary
MANDY: a modern form of Amanda
MANESSA: (Sans.) wise
MANNUELA: (Span.-Heb.) God is with us
MARABEL: (Fr.) beauteous Mary
MARCELLA: (Teut.) a semi-precious pink stone, named after St Marcel of Piedmont; feminine form of Marcellus
MARCIA: (Latin) brave, derived from god Mars
MARELLA: (Heb.-Teut.) Mary of bright intellect
MARG, MARGOT: short form of Margaret – a pearl
MARGARET: (Gr.) a pearl
MARGARETE: a Swiss form of Margaret

MARGARITA: a Spanish form of Margaret

MARGERY, MARJORIE: other forms of Margaret

MARIA: Latin form of Mary. Universal throughout Europe; came into fashion in England in eighteenth century

MARIAN, MARIANNE, MARY-ANN: a compound of Mary and Anne

MARIBELLE: (see Marabel)

MARIE: French form of Mary

MARIEL: (Teut.) spiritual

MARIETTA: Italian diminutive of Mary – wished-for child

MARIGOLD(E): (Teut.) Mary's gold; (Ang.-Sax.) resplendent Mary

MARINA: (Lat.) maiden of the sea

MARISA: (Lat.) sea-lover

MARLEE: (Gr.) guarded

MARLENE: (Heb.) of Magdala

MARMORA: (Gr.) radiant

MARNIE: (Heb.) storyteller

MAROLA: (Lat.) she who lives by the sea

MARSHA: a variant of Marcia – brave

MARTA: (Dan.) treasure

MARTHA: (Arab.) a lady

MARTINA: feminine form of Martin

MARTINE: (Fr.) combative

MARVA: (Lat.) wonderful

MARY: (Heb.) wished-for child. The name of the Blessed Virgin, and as such was once considered too sacred for common use; first found as Christian name in England at end of twelfth century

MARYAM: (Arab.) form of Miriam – sadness

MARYLYN: (Heb.) of Mary's line

MASHA: (Rus.) much-wanted child

MASON: (Fr.) reliable; diligent

MATHILDA, MATILDA: (Teut.) mighty battle-maid; heroine

MATRONNA: (Lat.) motherly
MATSU: (Jap.) pine tree
MATTA: (Heb.) gift of the Lord
MAUD, MAUDE: contractions of Matilda
MAURA: (Lat.) dark
MAUREEN: (Celt.) dark; also Irish form of Mary
MAURILLA: (Teut.) wise, dark-eyed girl
MAURITA: (Lat.) little dark girl
MAVIS: (Celt.) the song-thrush
MAXENTIA: (Lat.) of great talent
MAXIMA: (Lat.) greatest
MAY: (Teut.) the month; a maiden; a nineteenth-century pet-form of Margaret
MAYA: (Span.) hardworking; one of a kind
MAYBELLE: (Teut.) beautiful May
MAYNA: (Teut.) home woman
MAYRA: (Span.) creative; flourishing
MAZEL: (Heb.) lucky
MEAGAN: (Irish) joyful; precious
MEDARDA: (Heb.) pearl of wisdom; (Lat.) scholar
MEDEA: (Gr.) the enchantress; she who rules
MEDIA: (Lat.) the centre
MEDITA: (Lat.) reflective
MEDORA: (Gr.) guardian; (Ang.-Sax.) patient wife
MEERA: (Hin.) rich
MEG: an English contraction of Margaret
MEGAN: (Lat.) great
MEHETABEL, MEHITABEL: (Heb.) God benefits
MEINGOLDA: (Teut.) my golden flower
MEINWEN: (Wel.) slender
MELADA: (Gr.) honey
MELANIE: (Lat.) black, or one in black – a mourner
MELANTHA: (Gr.) dark or melancholy flower
MELEDA: (Teut.) chatterer
MELIA: (Gr.) the ash-tree
MELIANTHA: (Gr.) sweet flower

MELIKA: (Gr.) lyrical
MELINA: (Gr.) gentle; (Lat.) honey-sweet
MELINDA: (Lat.) honey
MELISANDE: (Fr.) strong
MELISSA: (Gr.) bee, a symbol of industry
MELITA: (Lat.) sweet as honey; (Gr.) little honey flower
MELLIE: (Gr.) sweet
MELLITA: (Gr.) honeyed
MELODY: (Gr.) musical
MELONIA: (Gr.) dark
MELORA: (Lat.) good
MELOSA: (Gr.) melody
MELROSE: (Eng.) sweet child; honey of roses
MELVA: (Celt.) chief
MELVINA: a variant form of Melva
MENA: (Lat.) mercy; (Egyp.) pretty
MERARI: (Gr.) she of sadness
MERAS: (Heb.) worthy
MERCEDES: (Lat.) a pleasing reward; (Span.) merciful
MERCY: compassion; a popular Puritan name
MEREDITH: (Celt.) sea-protector
MERIDA: (Lat.) noonday
MERIEL: (Gr.) a variant of Muriel – fragrant, perfumed
MERLE: (Lat.) a blackbird
MERRIE: (Ang.-Sax.) mirthful
MERRILA: (Gr.) fragrance
MERRILL: (Irish) shining
MERULA: (Lat.) blackbird
MERYL: (Gr.) the fragrant myrrh
META: (Lat.) a goal; turning point in a race
MIA: (Ital.-Span.) mine
MICAH: (Heb.) God-loving
MICHAELA: (Heb.) she who is like a goddess; divine
MICHELLE: (It.-Fr.) like the Lord; feminine form of Michael
MIGNON: (Fr.) cute
MIGNON: (Lat.) delicate; (Old Fr.) delicately formed
MIHEWI: (N.A. Ind.) sun-woman
MILBURGA: (Teut.) mild pledge

MILDRED: (Gr.) mild power
MILEY: modern usage meaning radiant
MILLICENT: (Lat.) sweet singer; (Gr.) goddess of moisture
MILLIE: English contraction of Millicent
MIMI: (Teut.) resolute opponent
MINA: pet-name for Wilhelmina
MINDORA: (Teut.) love's gift
MINERVA: (Lat.) the wise one
MINNA: (Teut.) love; memory
MINNIE: (Teut.) remembrance; Scottish form of Mary
MIONE: (Gr.) small
MIRA, MYRA: (Slav.) peace; (Gr.) she who weeps
MIRABEL, MIRABELLA, MIRABELLE: (Lat.) of great beauty
MIRANDA: (Lat.) admirable
MIRIAM: (Heb.) exalted; wished-for child
MIRU: (Slav.) harmony, peace
MITA: (Slav.) the day
MITZI: pet form of Mary and Maria
MO: (Irish) diminutive of Maureen
MOCITA: (Sans.) set free
MODANA: (Sans.) gladdening
MODESTA: (Lat.) modest
MODWEN, MODWENNA: (Wel.) maiden; queen
MOIRA: (Gr.) destiny; (Celt.) gentle
MOLL, MOLLIE, MOLLY: English contractions of Mary
MONA: (Teut.) lonely, or remote; (Lat.) celibate
MONICA: (Lat.) advisor
MORA: (Gael.) sun
MORGAN: (Wel.) girl on the shore
MORIA: (Gr.) chosen by the Lord or fate
MORNA: (Celt.) beloved
MORWENNA: (Wel.) maiden of the sea

MOTO: (Jap.) source
MOYNA: (Celt.) the gentle and soft
MOZA: (Heb.) fountain
MURIEL: (Gr.) fragrant, perfume; the myrrh
MUSA: (Lat.) a song
MUSETTA: (Lat.) a little song
MUSIDORA: (Gr.) gift of the muses
MYFANWY: (Wel.) my rare one
MYLENE: (Gr.) girl with dark skin
MYRA: (see Mira)
MYRNA: modern usage
MYRTLE: (Gr.) token of victory

N

NAAMA: (N.A. Ind.) pleasantness
NAARAH: (Heb.) girl of our hearts
NABILA: (Arab.) noble
NACARENA: (Span.) reborn
NADA: (Sans.) a species of reed
NADIA: (Slav.) hopeful
NADINE: (Slav.) hope
NADIRA: (Arab.) precious gem
NAGIDA: (Heb.) thriving
NAHAMA, NAHAMAN: (Heb.) God's comfort
NAHTANHA: (N.A. Ind.) corn flower
NAIDA: (Lat.) water nymph
NAKIA: (Arab.) pure girl
NAKITA: (Rus.) precocious
NALIN: (N.A. Ind.) serene
NAMI: (Jap.) wave
NAN: abbreviation of Nancy
NANCY: (Heb.) grace; another form of Anne
NANETTE: (Heb.) little graceful one; also French form of Nancy
NANINE: (Gr.) dainty little one
NAOMI: (Heb.) pleasantness, or pleasant one
NARA: (Gr.) happy
NARDA: (Gr.) the fragrant one; (Lat.) plant-name (spikenard from 'spicanardi')
NASHA: (Span.) a miracle

NATA: (Sans.) dancer
NATALIE: (Lat.) Christmas child
NATASHA: (Rus.) form of Natalie – Christmas child
NATHANIA: (Heb.) feminine form of Nathaniel
NATSU: (Jap.) summer
NAVEEN: (Span.) snowing
NEALA: (Gael.) feminine form of Neal – champion
NEBA: (Lat.) misty
NECIE: (Hung.) intense
NEDA: (Slav.) Sabbath-born
NEDRA: (Eng.) secretive
NEEMA: (Heb.) melodious
NELL, NELLIE, NELLY: variants of Ellen, Eleanor, or Helen
NEMERA: (Arab.) exotic
NENET: (Egyp.) goddess of the sea
NEOMA: (Gr.) the new moon
NERA: (Heb.) candlelight
NERIDA: (Gr.) sea-nymph
NERINE: (Gr.) sea-born; a flower
NERISSA: (Gr.) of the sea
NERYS: (Wel.) ladylike
NESSA: (Irish) devout
NESSIE: Welsh diminutive of Agnes
NESTA: a variant of Nessie
NETTA: (Gr.) the duckling; (Teut.) a net
NEVA: (Lat.) snow
NEVADA: (Lat.) snowy
NEYSA: (Gr.) chaste, pure
NIA: (Gr.) priceless
NIAMH: (Irish) promising
NICOLA, NICOLE: (Gr.) victor of the people; feminine form of Nicholas
NICOLETTE: (Gr.) victorious little one
NIDA: (Gr.) sweet girl
NIDIA, NYDIA: (Lat.) the homemaker
NIETA: (Span.) granddaughter
NIGELLA: (Lat.) plant-name; black
NIKITA: (Rus.) daring
NIMA: (Arab.) blessed
NINA: (Babylonian) in mythology, a goddess of the sea
NIPHA: (Gr.) a snowflake

NIRVANA: (Hin.) completeness
NITA: a Spanish contraction of Juanita
NIU: (Chin.) confident
NOA: (Heb.) chosen
NOELEEN: modern usage
NOELLA, NOELLE: (Teut.) the Nativity; born on Christmas Day
NOLA, NOLANA: (It.) a little bell
NOLETA: (Lat.) the unwilling maiden
NONA: (Lat.) ninth; the ninth child
NORA, NORAH: (Lat.) honour; Irish abbreviated form of Honora
NOREEN: Irish variant of Nora
NORIA: (Pers.) a water-wheel
NORIKA: (Jap.) athletic
NORINE: (Lat.) honourable
NORMA: origin obscure, but may have derived from Latin meaning exact to a pattern or precept. More generally used after Bellini's opera, *Norma* (1831)
NORNA: (Lat.-Scan.) a Norse fate (goddess)
NOURA: (Arab.) girl of light
NOVA, NOVIA: (Lat.) new
NUNCIATA: (Lat.) a form of Annunciata; messenger of a delightful promise
NYASSA: (Ang.-Sax.) sister; (Gr.) pierced
NYMPHODORA: (Gr.) gift of the nymphs; bride gift

O

OBALA: (Heb.) from the hills
OBELIA: (Gr.) a tall, pointed pillar
OCTAVIA: (Lat.) the eighth
ODA: (Teut.) rich; (Lat.) a song
ODALIS: (Span.) humorous
ODEDA: (Heb.) strength of character
ODELET, ODELETTE: (Gr.-Lat.) a little song
ODELIA: (Dan.) the heiress; (Teut.) prosperous
ODELITA: (Span.) singer

ODESSA: (Eng.) one on a great journey
ODETTE: (Teut.) heritage
ODINA: (N.A. Ind.) girl of the mountains
ODRA: (Eng.) affluent
OHARA: (Jap.) meditative
OILIEN: (Rus.) deer
OKSANA: (Rus.) praise to God
OLA: (Gr.) the virgin; (Heb.) eternal; (Scan.) daughter or descendant
OLATHE: (N.A. Ind.) beautiful
OLATTA: (N.A. Ind.) a lagoon
OLEDA: (Span.) audacious
OLENA: (Rus.) generous
OLETHEA: (Gr.) gift of the gods; (Lat.) of truth
OLGA: Russian name of Scandinavian origin, 'helga'
OLIDA: (Span.) light-hearted
OLINA: (Haw.) joy
OLINDA: (Lat.) fragrant
OLIVE, OLIVIA: (Lat.) the olive tree, symbol of peace; feminine form of Oliver
OLWEN: (Wel.) white footprint
OLYMPIA: (Gr.) of (Mt) Olympus; high, heavenly
OMA: (Heb.) reverent
OMORA: (Arab.) red-headed
ONA: (Lat.) a form of Una – the one
ONDINE: (see Undine)
ONEIDA: (N.A. Ind.) anticipated
ONYX: (Gr.) jewel-name
OONAH: (Celt.) Irish form of Una (Lat.) – the one; expressive of perfection
OPAL: (Sans.) jewel; most beautiful of gemstones
OPHELIA: (Gr.) one who helps
OPRAH: (Heb.) high-flyer
ORA: (Gr.) that of beauty; (Lat.) to pray, to orate
ORCHID: (Gr.) flower name
ORDRICK: (Teut.) of kingly origin
ORELLA: (Lat.) she who listens
ORIANA: (Celt.) girl of the

golden (or white) skin; (Lat.) risen
ORIN: (Irish) dark-haired
ORIOLA: (Lat.) the oriole
ORITHNA: (Gr.) natural
ORLA: (Irish) gold
ORLANTHA: (Teut.) of wide fame
ORLENA, ORLINE: (Fr.) the golden maiden; (Lat.) of golden radiance
ORTRUD: (Teut.) golden maid
ORVA: (Teut.) golden; (Ang.-Sax.) a brave friend
ORVALA: (Lat.) of golden worth
OSELLA: (It.) a bird
OSYTH: (Ang.-Sax.) war-god
OTHA: (Teut.) prosperous
OTILIA: (Slav.) fortunate
OTTA: (Ang.-Sax.) a mountain
OUIDA: modern usage, probably coined from nom-de-plume of once-popular novelist
OVINA: (Lat.) lamb-like
OWENA: (Wel.-Gr.) a feminine form of Owen – well-born
OWISSA: (N.A. Ind.) a blue-bird; harbinger of spring
OZELLA: (Heb.) a shadow

P

PACIFICA: (Lat.) peaceable
PADILLA: (Span.) loving
PADMA: (Hin.) lotus flower
PAGE, PAIGE: (Fr.) sharp; eager
PAISHA: (Slav.) wise
PAITON: (Eng.) sad
PALA: (N.A. Ind.) water
PALLAS: (Gr.) the wise maiden
PALLUA: (Heb.) distinguished
PALMEDA: (Gr.) inventive
PALOMA: (Span.) a dove
PAMELA: (Teut.) gift of the elf, suggesting intellect
PANDITA: (Hin.) wise, learned
PANDORA: (Gr.) all-gifted; universal gift
PANFILA: (Gr.) friendly

PANSY: (Gr.) remembrance
PANTHIA: (Gr.) divine
PANYA: (Gr.) crowned
PAOLA: (Span.) fiery
PARIS: (Fr.) place name; graceful
PARMINDER: (Hin.) attractive
PARTHA: (Gr.) pure
PARTHENIA: (Gr.) a virgin
PARVATI: (Hin.) child of the mountains
PASCHA: (Slav.) born at Easter
PAT, PATTIE, PATTY: (see Patricia)
PATIENCE: (Lat.) calm endurance
PATRICIA: (Lat.) of noble birth; feminine form of Patrick
PATSY: a diminutive of Patricia – of noble birth
PAULA: (Lat.) little; feminine form of Paul
PAULETTE: (Lat.) a little wee one
PAULINA, PAULINE: (Lat.) little one
PAVITA: (Sans.) purified
PAX: (Lat.) goddess of peace
PAXTON: (Lat.) peaceful
PAYTON: modern usage; aggressive
PEACE: (Lat.-Old Fr.) happy freedom; a peaceful child
PEARL: probably a variant of Latin word 'perula', pear; also coined after name of gem
PEGGY: Old English diminutive of Margaret
PELAGIA, PELAGIE: (Gr.) dweller by the sea
PELEKA: (Haw.) strong
PELHAM: (Eng.) thoughtful
PELIA: (Heb.) marvellous
PENELOPE: (Gr.) a weaver
PENTHEA: (Gr.) fifth; the fifth child
PEONY: (Gr.) flower name; probably named after Palon, physician to the gods
PEPITA: (Heb.) addition; (Span.) she who adds
PERDITA: (Lat.) lost
PERITA: (Span.) treasure
PERIZADA: (Pers.) fairy-born

PERLITA: (It.) pearl
PERNELLE: (Gr.) stone or rock
PERPETUA: (Lat.) perpetual
PERSEPHONE: (Gr.) the breath of spring
PERSIA: place name; colourful
PETRA: (Slav.) glamorous; capable
PETRINA: (Gr.-Lat.) stony
PETRONELLA: (Lat.) from the Gentile name Petronius
PETULA: (Lat.) seeker
PETUNIA: flower name; perky
PHALOSA: (Gr.) shining
PHEBE, PHOEBE: (Gr.) the shining one
PHEDRA: (Gr.) bright child
PHENICE: (Heb.) of the stately palm tree
PHILANA: (Heb.) loving grace
PHILANTHA: (Gr.) lover of flowers
PHILIPPA: (Gr.) lover of horses
PHILLIDA, PHILLINE: (Gr.) a loving woman
PHILOMENA: (Gr.) I am loved; loving mind
PHILOTHRA: (Gr.) pious
PHILYRIA: (Gr.) grace of the willow
PHIRA: (Gr.) she who loves music
PHOENIX: (Gr.) reborn
PHOTINA, PHOTINE: (Gr.) light
PHRYNE: (Gr.) pale
PHYLLIS, PHILLIS, PHILLIDA: (Gr.) a leafy green bough
PIA: (Lat.) pious, devout
PIERETTE: a French diminutive of Pierre (Peter) – rock
PILAR: (Lat.) tall and strong (like a pillar)
PINON: (Gr.) pearl
PIPER: (Eng.) one who plays the pipe
PIPPA: an Italian diminutive of Philippa – lover of horses
PIXIE: modern usage; small; zany
PLACIDA: (Lat.) calm

POLL, POLLY: variants of Mary
POMONA: (Lat.) the delicious fruit; goddess of fruit
POPPY: (Old Eng.) after flower
PORTIA: (Lat.) meaning obscure; some references give it as harbour-safety, others porcine
POSY: modern usage; sweet
PRECIOSA: (Lat.) precious
PREMA: (Hin.) love
PRIMA: (Lat.) the first; often given to the first child of the family
PRIMALIA: (Lat.) spring-like
PRIMAVERA: (Lat.) fragrant promise of youth; born in springtime
PRIMROSE: (Lat.) first rose
PRISCILLA: (Lat.) old, indicating a long life
PRIYA: (Hin.) sweetheart; (Sans.) beloved
PROBA: (Lat.) honest
PRUDENCE: (Lat.) prudent
PRUNELLA: (Lat.) shy
PSYCHE: (Gr.) the soul, emphasizing the spiritual nature
PULCHERIA: (Lat.) of great beauty
PYRENE: (Gr.) red-haired
PYTHIA: (Gr.) the high priestess; Apollo's priestess at Delphi

Q

QUANDA: (Eng.) queenly
QUARTAS: (Lat.) the fourth (born)
QUEENA: (Teut.) consort of a king; female sovereign
QUEENIE: (Eng.) dignified; royal
QUENBY: (Scan.) womanly
QUENNA: (Eng.) feminine
QUERIDA: (Span.) the loved one
QUESTA: (Lat.) the plaintive song (note) of the nightingale
QUILLA: (Eng.) writer
QUINBY: (Scan.) one who lives like royalty

QUINTA, QUINTELLA, QUINTINA: (Lat.) the fifth

QUINTESSA: (Lat.) essential goodness

QUINTILLA: (Lat.) the fifth girl; a Roman prophetess

QUITA: (Lat.) peaceful

QUITERIA: (Lat.) vital

R

RABIA: (Arab.) wind

RACHAEL, RACHEL: (Heb.) a ewe or ewe lamb

RACHELLE: (Fr.) calm

RACINDA: (Slav.) peaceful

RACQUEL: (Fr.) friendly

RADHA: (Hin.) successful

RADINKA: (Teut.) playful

RAE: a contraction of Rachel

RAELEAN, RAELEEN, RAELINE: modern usage; coined by someone with an ear for something prettily new, and borrowed by many in the 1960s

RAFAELA: (Heb.) spiritual

RAHMA: (Arab.) divine mercy

RAINE: (Lat.) a helpful friend

RAMONA: (Teut.) under judge's protection; also a Spanish name

RAMSAY: (Eng.) country girl

RANA: (Hin.) royal

RANDA: (Lat.) one who is admired

RAPHAELA: (Heb.) God's health

RASA: (Slav.) morning dew

RAVEN: (Eng.) a blackbird

RAYMA: (Teut.) rambler

RAZIA: (Heb.) secretive

REAGAN: modern usage; strong

REBA: a short form of Rebecca

REBECCA, REBEKAH: possibly from Hebrew word meaning 'heifer'; other authorities give meaning as peace-maker, and one of enchanting beauty

REDENTA: (Lat.) redeemed
REENIE: (Gr.) peace-loving
REESE: modern usage; trend-setter
REGINA: (Lat.) queen; (Teut.) purity, purified. Revived in England in nineteenth century
REI: (Jap.) ceremonious
REIKO: (Jap.) appreciative
REMAH: (Heb.) pale beauty
REMI: (Fr.) girl from Rheims
RENATA: (Lat.) born again
RENEE: (Fr.) born again
RENITA: (Lat.) resistance
RENNAH: (Heb.) a ringing cry
RESEDA: (Lat.) dainty and graceful
REVA: (Lat.) she who has been restored; (Old Fr.) a dreamer
REXANA: (Lat.-Heb.) regal grace
RHEA: (Gr.) she flows with honey and delight
RHIALL: (Irish) nymph
RHIANNON: (Wel.) intuitive; also a goddess
RHODA: (Gr.) a rose
RHONA: (Celt.) wielding power
RIA: (Span.) water-loving
RICARDA: (Lat.-Teut.) powerful; a woman fit for a king
RIDA: (Arab.) satisfied
RIHANNA: (Scan.) nymph
RILEY: (Irish) courageous; lively
RINA: (Gr.) pure; probably also variant of Rinnah
RINNAH: (Heb.) a ringing cry
RISSA: (Lat.) laughing
RITA: (Sans.) brave, honest; also contraction of Margaret and Margarita
RIVA: (Heb.) sparkling
RIVER: (Lat.) woman by the stream
RIZA: (Gr.) dignified
ROANNA: (Heb.-Teut.) gracious
ROBERTA: (Teut.) bright flame; feminine form of Robert
ROBIA: (Teut.) famous
ROBIN: (Eng.) bird name; taken by the wind

ROBINA: (Teut.) a variant of Roberta – bright flame

ROCHANA: (Pers.) dawn of day

ROCHEEN: (Fr.) sturdy

ROCHELLE: (Fr.-Heb.) small but strong-willed

RODERICA: (Teut.) feminine form of Roderic(k) – rich in fame

ROHAN, ROHANA: (Heb.) sandalwood

ROLANDA: (Teut.) feminine form of Roland – fame of the land

ROMA: (Romany) a gipsy; also Italian spelling of city of Rome

ROMAINE: (Fr.) daring

ROMILDA: (Teut.) little brave battle-maid

ROMOLA: (Lat.) a Roman lady

RONA: (Scan.) powerful

ROSA: Latinized version of Rose

ROSABEL, ROSABELLE: (Lat.) the beautiful rose

ROSALEEN: (Lat.) noble rose

ROSALIE: (Lat.) little rose

ROSALIND, ROSALINDA, ROSALINE: variants of Rose

ROSAMUND: (Teut.) horse-protection; (Lat.) rose of the world

ROSANNE: (Lat.-Heb.) rose of grace

ROSARANA: (Celt.) the rose-bush

ROSE, ROSIE: origin obscure, although thought to have derived from '(h)ros', or horse, and introduced into England by the Normans in the form of Roese; for centuries identified with the flower

ROSELLE: (Lat.) little rose

ROSEMARIE: a variant of Rosemary

ROSEMARY: (Lat.-Heb.) Mary's rose; dew of the sea

ROSETTA: (Lat.) little rose

ROSGRANA: (Celt.) sunbeam

ROWENA: (Celt.) white-bosomed

ROXANA, ROXANE: (Pers.) dawn of day
ROZENE: (N.A. Ind.) rose
RUBY: a gem; thought to have derived from Rupert, meaning bright flame
RUCITA: (Sans.) glittering
RUELLA: (Teut.) lucky elfin one
RUFINA: (Lat.) reddish; red-haired
RUMER: (Eng.) unique
RUTH: origin obscure; may have derived from Hebrew word meaning a vision; first used in England after the Reformation

S

SABBA: (Heb.) rest
SABELLA: (Lat.) the wise
SABINA: (Lat.) a Sabine woman (the Sabines of ancient Italy dwelt in mountains beyond the Tiber)
SABLA: (Arab.) young
SABRINA: (Old Eng.) legendary daughter of Loerine, mythical king of England
SACHA: (Gr.) helpful girl
SACHARISSA: (Gr.) sweet
SACHIN: (Slav.) lucky
SADHANA: (Hin.) loyal
SADIE: an English pet-name for Sarah
SAFFRON: modern usage; a spice
SAFIA: (Arab.) pure
SAGE: (Lat.) wise
SAHILA: (Hin.) guide
SAI: (Jap.) intelligence
SAIDA: (Heb.) happy girl
SALIH: (Arab.) virtuous
SALIMA: (Arab.) healthy
SALLY: an English contraction of Sarah, but has become an independent name
SALMA: (Heb.-Span.) peaceful
SALOME: (Heb.) peaceable
SALVINA: (Lat.) the sage flower; symbol of caution
SAMALA: (Sans.) tranquilizing

SAMANTHA: (Heb.) good listener
SAMARA: (Lat.) seed of the elm; (Heb.) the gentle guardian
SAMIA: (Hin.) joyful
SAMIRA: (Arab.) charismatic
SANCHA: (Span.) sacred child
SANCHIA: (Span.) holy
SANDRA: a derivative of Alexandra and Cassandra
SANNA: (Scan.) truthful
SANTA: (Lat.) saint
SANYA: (Slav.) dreamer
SAPPHIRA: (Heb.) the pretty one
SARA(H): (Heb.) princess
SARAID: (Celt.) excellent; used in Ireland
SARI: (Heb.-Arab.) noble
SASHA: (Rus.) helpful; courtesan
SASKIA: origins obscure; probably Dutch, evolved from the old German 'sachs', meaning Saxon
SATYA: (Arab.) lucky
SAVANNAH: (Ang.-Sax.) a treeless plain
SCARLETT: (Eng.) red
SCOUT: (Fr.) precocious
SEANA: (Irish) giving
SECUNDA: (Lat.) the second (child)
SEDA: (Arm.) echo through the woods
SELA: (Gr.) the shining one
SELDA: (Teut.) sure-footed
SELENA, SELINA: (Gr.) the moon, moonlight
SELMA: (Celt.) fair
SEMELE: (Lat.) the one and only; (Gr.) mythical daughter of Cadmus and Hermione, whose graceful beauty aroused Juno's jealous rage
SENONE: (Span.) energetic
SEPTIMA: (Lat.) seventh (child)
SERAFINA: (Heb.) ardent
SERENA: (Lat.) tranquil, calm
SERICA: (Lat.) silken
SHADA: (N.A. Ind.) the pelican
SHAE: (Heb.) shy

SHAELA: (Irish) pretty
SHAKIRA: (Span.-Arab.) grateful
SHAMARA: (Arab.) assertive
SHANA: (Heb.) pretty girl
SHANNA: (Irish) lovely
SHANNON: (Irish) clever
SHARITA: (Fr.) charitable
SHARON: (Heb.) open-hearted
SHAY: (Irish) place where fairies dwell
SHEBA: (Heb.) bound by the vows of faithfulness
SHEDEA: (N.A. Ind.) wild sage
SHEELAGH, SHEILA: Irish forms of Cecilia
SHELBY: (Eng.) dignified
SHELLEY: (Eng.) enjoys the outdoors
SHEREE: (Fr.) dear girl
SHERRY: (Fr.) outgoing
SHERYL: (Teut.) a variant of Shirley – meadow; sweet
SHILOH: (Heb.) a gift from God
SHIRLEEN: (Pers.) sweet
SHIRLEY: (Teut.) meadow; sweet
SHOHAN: (Heb.) pearl
SHOLA: (Heb.) spirited
SHONA: (Irish) open-hearted
SIAN: (Wel.) believer
SIBYL: (Cr.) a wise woman
SIDA: (Gr.) a water-lily
SIDNEY: place name, from Saint-Denis in France
SIDONIE: (Fr.) appealing
SIDRA: (Lat.) star
SIENNA: (Eng.) delicate; red-brown
SIERRA: place name, meaning with peaks
SIGOURNEY: (Eng.) conqueror
SIGRID: (Teut.) conquering counsellor
SILVIA, SYLVIA: (Lat.) forest dweller
SIMCHA: (Heb.) joyful
SIMONE: (Fr.) wise; thoughtful
SINEAD: (Irish) singer
SIOBHAN: (Irish) believer; lovely
SIREN, SIRENE: (Gr.) sorceress, enchantress
SITA: (Hin.) divine
SKYE: (Eng.) high-minded

SOFIA, SOFIE: (Gr.) wise
SOLAH: (Lat.) alone
SOLANA: (Span.) sunny
SOLITA: (Lat.) little lonely one
SOLVEIG: (Ice.) sunshine
SONDRA: (Gr.) defender of humankind
SONIA: (Slav.) wise one; a Russian form of Sophia – wisdom
SONYA: (Gr.) wise
SOPHIA, SOPHIE: (Gr.) wisdom
SORAYA: (Pers.) royal
SOREL: (Fr.) red-brown
STACEY: (Gr.) a variant of Anastasia – resurrection
STELLA: (Lat.) star-like
STEPHANIE: (Gr.) a crown
SUKI: (Jap.) beloved
SULA: (Ice.) the sun
SULWYN: (Wel.) fair as the sun
SUMMER: (Eng.) fresh; summery
SUNDAY: (Lat.) day name
SUNILA: (Hin.) blue sky
SURI: (Heb.) princess
SUSAN(NAH): (Heb.) white lily
SUZETTE: (Heb.) little lily
SWETLANA: (Teut.) a star
SYBIL: (Gr.) a wise woman
SYDNEY: (Fr.) enthusiastic
SYLVA: (Lat.) woodland
SYLVANA: (Lat.) of the woodland
SYLVIA: (see Sibyl)

T

TABITHA: (Aramaic) graceful gazelle; (Syrian) gazelle
TACEY: modern usage; precious
TACITA: (Lat.) the silent one
TADITA: (N.A. Ind.) runner
TAHIRA: (Arab.) pure
TAIMA: (N.A. Ind.) thunder
TAKA: (Jap.) honourable
TAKI: (Jap.) waterfall
TAKIA: (Arab.) spiritual
TALI: (Heb.) confident
TALIA: (Gr.) golden
TALITHA: (Arab.) graceful

as the gazelle; (Arm.) fair damsel
TALLULAH: (N.A. Ind.) restless as running water
TALMA: (Heb.) hill
TAMARA: (East Indian) aspiration
TAMASINE: (Eng.) twin; feminine
TAMIA: (Jap.) little gem
TAMSIN: (Eng.) benevolent
TANA: (Slav.) little princess
TANGELIA: (Gr.) angel
TANIA: a pet form of Tatiana
TANRIK: (Hin.) flowers
TANSY: (Lat.) pretty
TANYA: (Rus.) regal
TAPIA: (Span.) small
TARA: (Gael.) towering
TARINA: (Slav.) kind
TASHKA: (Rus.) together
TATE: (Eng.) short
TATIANA: (Lat.) silver-haired
TATUM: (Eng.) high-spirited, cheerful
TAYLOR: (Eng.) a tailor; trend-setter
TEAH: (Gr.) goddess
TEDRA: (Gr.) gregarious
TEGAN: (Wel.) beautiful
TELA: (Gr.) wise
TEMIRA: (Heb.) tall
TERAH: (Lat.) child of the earth
TERESA, THERESA: (Gr.) reap; a carrier of corn
TERESE: (Teut.) huntress
TERI: (Gr.) reaper
TERRENA: (Lat.) of earthly pleasures
TERTIA: (Lat.) third (child)
TESS(A): (see Terese)
THADA: (Gr.) appreciative
THALIA: (Gr.) luxuriant bloom
THEA: (Gr.) divine; a contraction of Theodora
THECLA: (Gr.) divine fame
THELMA: (Gr.) a nursling
THEODORA: feminine form of Theodore
THEODOSIA: (Gr.) divinely given
THEOLA: (Gr.) deified; sent from God
THEONE: (Gr.) serene

THERA: (Gr.) the untamed; the phallically unconquered
THERNA: (Gr.) wild
THETIS: (Gr.) a sea nymph; in mythology the mother of Achilles
THIA: (Gr.) goddess
THIRZA: (Heb.) pleasantness
THOMASA, THOMASINA: (Arm.) a twin
THORA: (Teut.) born of thunder
THYRA: (Teut.) belonging to Tyr, the Scandinavian god of battles
TIA: (Gr.-Span.) princess
TIANA: (Gr.) greatest beauty
TIBERIA: (Lat.) majestic
TIERNEY: (Irish) wealthy
TIFFANY: (Gr.) divine manifestation
TILDA, TILLIE, TILLY: (Teut.) variants of Mathillda, Matilda – mighty battle-maid
TINA: (Lat.) small lively one
TIRI: (Wel.) sweet
TISHA: (Lat.) joyful
TITA: (Lat.) safe
TONIA: (Lat.) wonderful; daring
TOPAZ: (Lat.) gemstone; sparking
TORA: (Scan.) dedicated to Thor, god of thunder
TRACEY, TRACY: from the surname
TRELLA: (Span.) sparkling star
TRICIA: (Lat.) humorous
TRINA: (Gr.) woman of purity
TRINETTE: (Gr.) little girl of purity
TRINITY: (Lat.) triad
TRISTA: (Lat.) the sorrowful one
TRIX, TRIXIE: contractions of Beatrice or Beatrix
TRUDY: (Eng.) contraction of Gertrude
TRYPHENA: (Gr.) daintiness, delicacy
TULA: (N.A. Ind.) moon

U

UDA: (Teut.) rich
UDELE: (Teut.-Ang.-Sax.) prosperous; the clever one
ULA: (Celt.) jewel of the sea
ULANI: (Haw.) happy
ULMA: (Lat.) the elm tree
ULRICA: (Teut.) noble ruler; rich
ULTIMA: (Lat.) the last
UMA: (Sans.) light
UMMA: (Hin.) mother
UNA: (Lat.) the one, expressive of perfection
UNDINE: (Lat.) of the waves; a water-sprite that can obtain a human soul by bearing a child to a human husband
UNICE: (Gr.) victorious
UNITY: (Eng.) oneness
URANIA: (Gr.) heavenly; in mythology muse of astronomy, daughter of Jupiter and Mnemosyne
URBANA: (Lat.) a polite, town-bred woman
URBI: (Egyp.) princess
URENA: (Slav.) one who lights the way
URIELA: (Heb.) God's light
URSA: (Lat.) of distinguished quality; the she-bear
URSULA: (Lat.) a variant of Ursa
UTA: (Teut.) battle heroine
UTINA: (N.A. Ind.) (woman of) my country
UTOPIA: (Eng.) idealistic
UZIA: (Heb.) God is my strength

V

VALDA: (Teut.) inspiring in battle
VALENTINA: (Lat.) the strong and valorous one
VALERIE: (Lat.) valiant, strong
VALLIE: (Lat.) natural
VALMAI: (Wel.) mayflower
VALONIA: (Lat.) a maiden of the valley; (Gr.) seed of the oak
VALORA: (Lat.) intimidating
VANDA: (Teut.) kindred

VANDANA: (Sans.) worship
VANESSA: (Gr.) a butterfly
VANIA: (Heb.) gifted; Russian equivalent of Jane
VANITA: (Sans.) wished for, desired
VANORA: (Celt.) white wave
VARDA: (Heb.) rosy
VASHTI: (Pers.) the best, the most beautiful
VAUGHAN: (Wel.) little one
VEDA: (Sans.) the learned and wise one
VEGA: (Scan.) star
VELMA: (Eng.) determined protector
VENETIA: (Lat.) blessed
VENUS: (Lat.) the Roman goddess of love
VERA: (Lat.) truth; also Russian form of faith
VERDA: (Lat.) fresh and virginal
VERINA: origin obscure; probably a variant of Vera (Lat.) truth; (Rus.) faith
VERITY: (Lat.) truth
VERNA: (Lat.) vernal, pertaining to spring
VERNITA: (Lat.) little blooming one
VERONA: (Lat.) the truthful
VERONICA: (Lat.-Gr.) true image
VESTA: (Gr.) same as Hestia; goddess of fire and of the family hearth
VICTORIA: (Lat.) victorious; feminine form of Victor
VIDA: (Heb.) beloved; (Lat.) life
VIDYA: (Sans.) knowledge
VINA: (Lat.) wine of life
VIOLA: (see Violante)
VIOLANTE: (Lat.) the violet, symbol of modesty
VIOLET: (Lat.) modest grace
VIOLETTA: (Lat.) little violet
VIRGINIA: (Lat.) a maid, virgin
VITA: (Lat.) vital; full of life
VIVIA: (Lat.) lively
VIVIAN: (Lat.) animated
VIVIENNE: French form of Vivian

VOLETA, VOLETTA: (Old Fr.) veil; the veiled woman

W

WAFA: (Arab.) loyal

WAHKUNA: (N.A. Ind.) beautiful

WAHLENE: (Teut.) chosen

WAKANA: (Jap.) thriving

WANDA: (Teut.) shepherdess

WASHINA: (N.A. Ind.) good health

WENDELIN: (Ang.-Sax.) the wanderer

WENDY: origin obscure; probably from Gwendolen (Celt.) meaning white-bow

WENONA, WENONAH, WINONA: (N.A. Ind.) the first-born daughter

WESLA: (Old Eng.) the girl from the west meadow

WETA: (Frie.) knowledge

WHITNEY: (Eng.) fresh; white

WILDA: (Ang.-Sax.) the wild one

WILHELMINA: (Nor.) the helmet

WILLA: (Teut.) resolute

WILLOW: willow tree; free spirit

WINEMA: (N.A. Ind.) chieftainess

WINIFRED: (Teut.) friend of peace

WINNY: (Celt.) famine; (Teut.) friend

WINOLA: (Teut.) friendly princess

WINSOME: (Eng.) pleasantly attractive

WYANET: (N.A. Ind.) of great beauty

WYLDA: (Teut.) wayward

WYLMA: (Teut.) resolute contender

WYNNE: (Wel.) fair, blessed; (Teut.) the fulfilled wish

X

XANTHE: (Gr.) yellow; the yellow-haired

XARA: (Heb.) variant of Sarah, meaning princess
XAVERIE: (Arab.) bird
XENA, XENE: (Gr.) a woman guest
XIMENA: (Gr.) listening
XYLIA: (Gr.) of a wood
XYLINA: (Gr.) wood dweller
XYLONA: (Gr.) wood or forest dweller

Y

YAFFA: (Heb.) lovely
YANA: (Slav.) lovely
YASMIN: a variant of Jasmine
YEDDA: (Teut.) singer
YELENA: (Rus.) friendly; (Gr.) bright; chosen one
YETTA: (Heb.) mistress of the house
YOLANDE: French form of Yolante (Gr.) violet of the land
YOSHE: (Jap.) a beauty
YSEULT, ISOLT: (Celt.) a picture fair
YSIDORA: (Gr.) fair gift
YVETTE: (Teut.) little ivy vine
YVONNE: (Heb.) grace of the Lord. French feminine of Ivon

Z

ZADAH: (Arab.) prosperous
ZADIE: (Arab.) affluent
ZAFIRA: (Arab.) successful
ZAMIRA: (Heb.) song
ZANA: (Pers.) woman
ZANETA: (Heb.) the grace of God
ZARA(H): (Arab.) brightness of the East; sunrise
ZAREBA: (Sud.) an enclosure
ZELDA: a form of Griselda
ZELLA: (Heb.) a shadow
ZELOSA: (Gr.) jealous
ZENA: (Pers.) a woman
ZENOBIA: (Arab.) her father's ornament
ZERLINDA: (Heb.-Lat.) a beautiful dawn
ZETA: (Gr.) a dwelling-place

ZILLAH: (Heb.) a shadow
ZIONA: (Heb.) a hill
ZITA: (Heb.) respected mistress
ZIVANA: (Slav.) animate
ZOE: (Gr.) life
ZORA: (Arab.) dawn
ZULEIKA: (Pers.) brilliant beauty

BOYS' NAMES

A

AAHMES: (Egyp.) child of the moon
AARON: (Heb.) lofty mountain; inspired; descended from the gods
ABBOT: (Heb.) father of many; the male head of an abbey
ABDIEL: (Heb.) God's servant
ABDULLAH: (Arab.) servant of Allah
ABE, ABY: contractions of Abraham
ABEL: (Heb.) a breath, vapour; vanity; second son of Adam and Eve
ABELARD: (Teut.) of noble firmness
ABIAH, ABIJAH: (Heb.) my father is the Lord
ABIEL: (Heb.) father of strength
ABIEZA: (Heb.) my father's help
ABITAL: (Heb.) father of the dew
ABNER: (Heb.) father of light
ABRAHAM: (Heb.) father of a multitude; originally Abram, high father
ABRIC: (Teut.) beyond authority
ABROS: (Gr.) elegant
ABSALOM: (Heb.) father of peace
ACE: (Eng.) the best; number one
ACHATES: (Gr.) faithful companion
ACHILLE: French form of Achilles
ACHILLES: (Gr.) without lips; Greek hero and central figure of Homer's *Iliad*
ACHIM: (Heb.) God will establish
ACIMA: (Heb.) the Lord will judge

ACKERLEY: (Old Eng.) from the oak-tree meadow
ADAIR: (Celt.) the oak-tree ford
ADAL: (Teut.) noble
ADAM: (Heb.) red earth man; first man
ADDIS: (Heb.-Eng.) an old contrived form of Adam
ADDISON: (Heb.) Adam's descendant
ADDO: (Teut.) noble cheer
ADELARD: (Teut.) noble eagle
ADELBERT: (Teut.) nobly bright
ADELFRID: (Teut.) noble; peaceful
ADELGAR: (Teut.) bright or noble spear
ADELPHO: (Gr.) beloved brother
ADELWIN: (Teut.) noble friend
ADEN: (Gael.) fire
ADIEL: (Heb.) an ornament of God
ADIN: (Heb.) voluptuous
ADITYA: (Sans.) belonging to the sun
ADLAI: (Heb.) my ornament
ADLAR: (Teut.) an eagle
ADMETUS: (Teut.) untamed
ADNA: (Heb.) pleasure
ADOETTE: (N.A. Ind.) big tree
ADOLF, ADOLPH: (Teut.) noble wolf
ADOLPHUS: Latin form of Adolf
ADONIS: (Gr.) adorned, of manly beauty; in mythology a hunter loved by Venus
ADRAH: (Heb.) ruler, prince
ADRASTUS: (Lat.-Gr.) capable
ADRIAN: (Lat.) of Adria
ADRIEL: (Heb.) one of God's flock
AELHAEARN: (Wel.) iron brow
AENEAS: (Gr.-Lat.) to praise; hero of Virgil's *Aeneid*
AGAR: (Heb.) stranger
AGATHON: (Gr.) famed for kindness and goodness

AGILO: (Lat.) gleaming
AGNAR: (Teut.) undefiled
AHAB: (Heb.) uncle
AHANU: (N.A. Ind.) one who laughs
AHEARN, AHERN: (Celt.) lord of the horses; (Wel.) iron
AHMED: (Arab.) more praiseworthy
AHRENS: (Teut.) power of the eagle
AIDAN: (Gael.) fire
AINSLEY: (Gael.) his own (ain) self
AIRELL: (Celt.) a free man
AJAX: (Gr.) earthy
AJAY: (Sans.) unconquerable
AKEEM: (Arab.) wise; insightful
AKIO: (Jap.) bright man
AKIRA: (Jap.) intelligence
AKON: modern usage
AKULE: (N.A. Ind.) he looks up
ALAN, ALLAN: (Celt.) harmony; (Gael.) fair, handsome
ALAND: (Celt.) bright as the sun
ALANUS: (Lat.) cheerful; (Celt.) in harmony
ALARD: (Teut.) nobly stern
ALARIC: (Gothic) all ruler
ALASTAIR, ALISTAIR: (Gr.) avenger; original Gaelic Alasdair, also variant of Alister
ALAUDO: (Lat.) a lark
ALBAN: (Lat.) dawn of day; white
ALBER: (Teut.) agile of mind
ALBERIC: (Teut.) a ruler with bright, agile mind; elf-king
ALBERN: (Teut.) bear-like, brave
ALBERT: (Teut.) nobly bright
ALBIN: (Lat.) fair
ALBOR: (Lat.) dawn
ALBURN: (Lat.) pale
ALCANDER: (Gr.) manly
ALDEN: (Ang.-Sax.) old friend
ALDER: (Teut.) a tree of the genus Alnus
ALDIS: (Eng.) from the old house
ALDO: (Teut.) steady; (Heb.) a servant

ALDRED: (Teut.) mature counsel
ALDRIC: (Eng.) old king
ALDRIDGE: (Teut.) dweller on the high ridge
ALDWIN: (Ang.-Sax.) old friend
ALECK, ALEX, ALICK: contractions of Alexander
ALED: (Wel.) offspring
ALEM: (Arab.) one who has knowledge
ALEXANDER: (Gr.) defender; helper of men
ALEXIS: (Gr.) defender; helper
ALFIE: a diminutive of Alfred – mature counsel
ALFRED: (Teut.) counsellor
ALGAR: (Old Eng.) elf spear
ALGERNON: (Old Fr.) bearded
ALGY: contraction of Algernon
ALI: (Arab.) servant
ALISTER: (Gr.) avenger; defender of men
ALLAN: (see Alan)
ALLYN: (see Alan)
ALMER: (Arab.) a prince
ALMERICK: (Teut.) work ruler
ALMO: (Gr.) a river god
ALOIS: (Teut.) a form of Aloysius; famous warrior; sixteenth-century Spanish saint
ALONZO: (Teut.) friend of all
ALOYSIUS: (Teut.) famous warrior; sixteenth-century Spanish saint
ALPHA: (Gr.) the first letter of the Greek alphabet; first-born
ALPHARD: (Arab.) solitary
ALPHEUS: (Gr.) god of the river
ALPHONSO: (Teut.) eager for the fray; willing
ALPIN: (Lat.) high, lofty
ALROY: (Lat.) royal; (Span.) king
ALSTON: (Ang.-Sax.) noble stone
ALTON: (Old Eng.) old town
ALVA: (Lat.-Span.) white
ALVAN, ALVIN: (Teut.) beloved of all

ALVAR: (Ang.-Sax.) elf enemy or elf army
ALVER: (Lat.) complete truth
ALVERNON: (Teut.-Lat.) of the springtime
ALVIS: (Scan.) wise suitor
ALWARD: (Teut.) protector of all
ALWIN, ALWYN: variants of Alvan
ALWORTH: (Teut.) respected by all
AMADEUS: (Lat.) the loving deity
AMADIS: (Lat.-Fr.) God love
AMALA: (Sans.) stainless
AMANDUS: (Lat.) worthy of love
AMARI: (Heb.) given by God
AMBROSE: (Gr.) immortal
AMIN: (Sans.) fruitful
AMINTAS: (Gr.) helpful
AMIR: (Heb.) prince; treetop
AMMON: (Egyp.) the hidden one
AMORY: (Teut.) famous ruler
AMOS: (Gr.) bearer of burdens; courageous
AMPARO: (Span.) defence; protection
ANAKIN: modern usage, meaning warrior
ANARAWD: (Wel.) eloquent
ANATOLE: (Gr.) sunrise
ANCEL: (Teut.) godlike
ANDERS: (Scan.) courageous
ANDERSON: (Eng.) son of Andrew
ANDREW: (Gr.) manly; brave
ANDRIAS: (Gr.) courageous
ANDROS: (Gr.) manly
ANEURIN: (Wel.) of true gold
ANGEL: (Gr.) messenger
ANGUS: (Celt.) excellent virtue
ANGWYN: (Wel.) very handsome
ANIL: (Sans.) air; wind
ANOKI: (N.A. Ind.) actor
ANSELM: (Teut.) divine helmet; protection
ANSON: (Teut.) of divine

origin; (Ang.-Sax.) the son of Ann
ANTHONY, ANTONY: (Lat.) priceless; highly praised
ANTOL: (Hung.) estimable
ANTON: Slavonic form of Anthony
ARAMIS: (Lat.) swordsman
ARCHER: (Teut.) a bowman
ARCHIBALD: (Teut.) very bold; bold archer
ARCHIE: a diminutive of Archibald – bold
ARCO: (Lat.) an arch or arc
ARDAL: (Irish) great valour
ARDEN, ARDIN: (Lat.) eager; fervent
ARDILLO: (Span.) a squirrel
ARDITH: (Old Fr.) flashing, fiery
ARES: (Gr.) ruin; god of war and son of Zeus
ARI: (Teut.) eagle
ARIEL: (Heb.) lion of God
ARISTO: (Gr.) the best
ARISTOL: (Gr.) excellence
ARLAN: (Gael.) pledge, oath
ARLES: (Scan.) a pledge
ARLETH: (Gr.) forgetful
ARLIN: (Teut.) sea-bound
ARLIS: (Heb.) pledge
ARLO: (Span.) the barbary; (Old Eng.) the protected town
ARLYN: (Teut.) swift, like the cascade
ARMAND: (Teut.) a form of Herman; war or commanding man
ARMANDO: (Lat.) armed
ARMYN: (Teut.) a form of Armand
ARNO: (Lat.-Teut.) eagle
ARNOLD: (Teut.) strong as an eagle
ARNVID: (Teut.) eagle of the forest
ARON: (Gr.) exalted
ARTHUR: (Celt.) lofty, noble; (Cymric) bear man
ARUNDEL: (Teut.) of the dell of eagles
ARVIN: (Teut.) man of the people
ARVO: (Finn.) worth, value
ARWEN: (Wel.) fair; fine
ASA: (Heb.) healer

ASHER: (Heb.) blessed, fortunate; (Egyp.) evening
ASHLEY: (Old Eng.) the ash wood
ASHTON: (Eng.) settlement in the ash-grove
ASLAN: (Turk.) lion
ATHELSTONE, ATHELSTAN: (Teut.) noble jewel or stone
ATHERTON: (Teut.) dweller in the woodland
ATHMORE: (Teut.) dweller in the heathland
ATHOL: (Teut.) of noble ancestry; (Ang.-Sax.) noble stone
ATLEE: (Heb.) God is just
ATTICUS: (Lat.) man from Athens
AUBERT: (Teut.) fair ruler
AUBREY: (Lat.) fair chief
AUDEN: (Old Eng.) old friend
AUDLEY: (Teut.) undefined
AUDRIS: (Teut.) daring
AUDWIN: (Teut.) wealthy friend
AUGUSTIN, AUGUSTUS: (Lat.) venerable; consecrated
AURIGA: (Lat.) charioteer
AURYN: (Wel.) gold
AUSTIN: an English contraction of Augustin
AVERIA: (Teut.) assertive
AVILA: (Span.) audacious
AXEL: (Heb.) father is peace
AYDEN: (Gael.) little fire
AYLA: (Gr.) of the woodland
AYLER: (Wel.) nobly renowned
AYLETT: (Lat.) a sea swallow
AYLMER: (Teut.) of noble fame
AYLSWORTH: (Teut.) of great wealth
AYLWARD: (Teut.) formidable guard
AYLWIN: (Teut.) devoted friend
AYMON: (Teut.) ruler of the home
AZAL: (Heb.) the mountain's foundation
AZAR, AZARIAH, AZARIAS: (Heb.) whom the Lord helps
AZEL: (Heb.) noble

B

BADEN: (Teut.) battle
BAILEY: (Teut.) the man in possession; (Fr.) an enclosure
BAINBRIDGE: (Gael.) of the sea
BAIRD: (Celt.) a variant of bard (singer)
BALDEMAR: (Teut.) of princely fame
BALDRIC: (Teut.) a warrior's belt or sash, denoting a brave soldier or prince; bold rule
BALDWIN: (Teut.) bold friend
BALFOUR: (Gael.) pasture ground
BALIN: (Sans.) a soldier of distinction
BALTHAZAR: (Babylonian) protect the king; one of the biblical Wise Men
BALVINDER: (Hin.) merciful; compassionate
BANCROFT: (Teut.) bean croft; (Ang.-Sax.) from the bean field
BANNISTER: (Gr.) the wild pomegranate
BARACK: African derivative of Hebrew Baruch, meaning blessed
BARCA: (Pho.) lightning
BARDO: (Teut.) giant
BARKER: (Old Eng.) shepherd
BARLOW: (Celt.) a low branch; (Teut.) dweller on the boar's hill
BARNABAS: (Heb.) consoling son
BARNABY: Teutonic form of Barnabas
BARNARD: (Teut.) firm commander
BARNY: an Irish contraction of Bernard
BARON: (Old Eng.) young warrior
BARRET, BARRETT: (Teut.) of bear strength
BARRY: (Celt.) he who looks straight at the mark; good marksman
BARTH: (Old Eng.) a shelter

BARTHOLOMEW: (Heb.) son of furrows; farmer
BARTIMEUS: (Heb.) of honourable lineage
BARTON: (Ang.-Sax.) a farmer
BARTRAM: (Teut.) fortunate farmer
BARUCH: (Heb.) blessed
BASHIR: (Arab.) well-educated; wise
BASIL: (Gr.) kingly
BAXTER: (Teut.) a baker
BAYARD: (Old Fr.) reddish-brown; he of the red hair
BEAU: (Fr.) handsome
BEAUFORT: (Fr.) dweller in the fort
BEAUMONT: (Old Fr.) beautiful height; fair hill
BEAUREGARD: (Fr.) fair of view; handsome
BEAVIS: (Eng.-Fr.) ox
BECKETT: (Old Eng.) beehive
BEDE: (Celt.) life; (Ang.-Sax.) prayer
BEDWIN: (Wel.) birch-like
BELA: (Heb.) eloquent
BELDEN: (Teut.) from a beautiful valley
BELEN: (Gr.) an arrow
BELLAMY: (Lat.) beautiful friend
BELT: (Wel.) bright
BELTHAM: (Teut.) comely
BELVA: (Lat.) fair
BENEDICT: (Lat.) blessed
BENIAH: (Heb.) son of the Lord
BENJAMIN: (Heb.) son of my strength; son of my right hand
BENNETT: (Fr.-Lat.) form of Benedict, meaning blessed
BENSON: (Eng.) son of Ben
BENTLEY: (Ang.-Sax.) from the winding grassy meadow
BENTON: (Ang.-Sax.) from the moor or meadow
BENVENUTO: (Lat.) welcome
BERENGER: (Teut.) bear-spear
BERESFORD: dweller by the bear's ford
BERGEN, BERGIN: (Teut.) dweller on the mountain
BERKLEY: (Teut.) dweller at the birch meadow

BERMAN: (Teut.) bear-keeper
BERNARD: (Teut.) bold as a bear
BERT: contraction of Bertram, Albert, and Herbert
BERTHELM: (Ang.-Sax.) bright helmet
BERTHOLD: (Teut.) ruling in splendour
BERTRAM: (Teut.) illustrious one; bright raven
BERTWIN: (Teut.) illustrious friend
BETA: (Gr.) second letter of the Greek alphabet; second son
BEVAN: (Celt.) son of Evan
BEVERLEY: (Ang.-Sax.) from the beaver meadow
BEVIS: (Teut.) a bow
BEYNON: (Wel.) son of Eynon
BIDDULPH: (Teut.) commanding wolf
BILL, BILLY: contractions of William
BIMISI: (N.A. Ind.) slippery
BJORN: (Old Nor.) bear
BLAINE: (Old Eng.) a bubble
BLAIR: (Teut.) dweller on a plain; (Gael.) a battleground
BLAISE: (Lat.) babbler
BLAKE: (Teut.) bright, as opposed to pallid
BLAND: (Lat.) gentle
BLEDDIAN, BLEDDYN: (Wel.) little wolf
BLIGH: (Old Eng.) bliss
BOB: English and Scottish contraction of Robert
BODEL: (Teut.) a herald
BOHDAN: (Slav.) God's gift
BOLESLAV: (Slav.) much glory
BONA: (Celt.) a messenger
BONAR: (Lat.) good
BONIFACE: (Lat.) doer of good; benefactor
BORDEN: (Old Eng.) refrain of a song
BORIS: (Rus.) fighter
BOURKE: (Teut.) a stronghold
BOURNE: (Old Fr.) destiny
BOWEN: (Wel.) son of Owen
BOWMAN: (Old Eng.) archer

BOYCE: modern usage
BOYD: (Celt.) yellow-haired
BOYDELL: (Celt.) wise fair one
BOYLE: (Teut.) agitation
BRADEN: (Teut.) broad
BRADFORD: (Ang.-Sax.) from the broad ford
BRADLEY: (Teut.) dweller in a broad meadow
BRADY: (Gr.) slow
BRAM: a short form of Abraham
BRAMWELL, BRANWELL: (Eng.) place of brambles
BRAN: (Celt.) a raven
BRAND: (Teut.) a flaming sword
BRANDON: (Teut.) firebrand
BRANNON: (Gael.) raven
BRANT: (Teut.) a flaming ray
BRAYDEN: (Eng.) broad, wide
BRENDAN: (Teut.) aflame
BRENT: (Gr.) upright; (Ang.-Sax.) a steep hill
BRETT: (Gael.) upright
BREVIS: (Lat.) short; frugal
BREWSTER: (Old Eng.) one who brews
BRIAN, BRIANT, BRYAN: (Celt.) strong; (Gael.) in a position of dignity
BRICE: (Ang.-Sax.) breach
BRINSLEY: (Ang.-Sax.) Brin's meadow
BRION: (Gael.) nobly descended
BRISBANE: (Gael.) royal mount
BROCARD: (Teut.) badger's earth
BROCK: (Old Eng.) a badger
BRODERICK: (Teut.) the king's tormentor
BRODIE, BRODY: (Teut.) a goad
BROMWELL: (Teut.) dweller by the wild broom spring
BROOKLYN: modern usage; place name
BRUCE: (Old Fr.) from Bruys in Normandy; name of great Scottish hero (Robert)
BRUIN: (Dutch) brown
BRUNO: (Teut.) brown

BRUTUS: (Lat.) stupid
BRYAN: (see Brian)
BRYCE: (Celt.) rapid, speedy
BRYCHAN: (Wel.) speckled
BRYDEN: (Irish) strong one
BRYMER: (Ang.-Sax.) bright
BRYN: (Wel.) hill
BUCKLEY: (Ang.-Sax.) beech meadow
BUDD: (Cymric) rich, victorious
BURDEN: (Teut.) something carried
BURGESS: (Old Eng.) a free-man of the town
BURKE: (Teut.) a stronghold
BURL: (Ang.-Sax.) a short form of Burleigh – town meadow
BURNETT: (Old Fr.) brown
BURTON: (Teut.) a tackle used for rigging ships
BYRLE: (Teut.) a cup-bearer
BYRNE: (Ang.-Sax.) coat of mail
BYRON: (Old Eng.) at the byres

C

CABOT: origin obscure; possibly meaning to sail
CADE: (Eng.) round; lumpy
CADELL: (Celt.) battle spirit
CADEN: modern usage
CADEYRN: (Wel.) battle king
CADFAEL: (Wel.) battle metal
CADMAN: (Celt.) strong in battle
CADMUS: (Gr.-Pho.) eastern
CADOC: (Celt.) warlike
CADOGAN: (Wel.) little battle
CADOR: (Wel.) shield
CAERWYN: (Wel.) white fort
CAESAR: (Lat.) head of hair; after Roman emperor Julius Caesar
CAI: (Lat.) rejoice
CAIDEN: (Arab.) companion
CAIN: biblical brother of Abel

CALDWELL: (Teut.) dweller by the cold spring
CALEB: (Heb.) a dog, symbol of fidelity
CALHOUN: (Irish) from the forest
CALIX: (Gr.) very handsome
CALLAGHAN: (Irish) strife; contention
CALLUM, CALUM: (Lat.) dove
CALVERT: (Ang.-Sax.) keeper of the calf-herd
CALVIN: (Lat.) bold
CAMERON: (Gael.) crooked nose
CAMPBELL: (Gael.) brave man
CANTON: (Fr.) dweller of corner
CARADOC: (Celt.) beloved
CARBURY: (Celt.) charioteer
CARDEW: (Wel.) black fort
CAREW: (Cymric) castle near the water
CAREY: (Lat.) dear
CARL, KARL: Teutonic form of Charles
CARLETON, CARLTON: (Ang.-Sax.) peasant's farm
CARLOS: Spanish form of Charles
CARMINE: (Lat.) song
CARMODY: (Manx) God of arms
CARNEY: (Celt.) brave soldier
CAROLAN: (Celt.) champion
CAROLUS: Latin form of Charles
CARRICK: (Celt.) a rocky headland
CARROLL: (Celt.) melody
CARSON: modern usage
CARTER: (Eng.) one who transports materials
CARVEL: (Manx) a song
CARY: (Teut.) walnut tree
CASEY: (Gael.) alert
CASPAR: (Pers.) a horseman
CASSIUS: (Lat.) empty; hollow
CASTOR: (Lat.) beaver
CATHAL: (Celt.) eye of battle
CATO: (Lat.) sagacious

CAVANAGH, CAVANAUGH: (Celt.) handsome
CAVELL: (Teut.) active and bold
CEBAS: (Gr.) reverence
CEBERT: (Teut.) bright
CECIL: (Lat.) blind
CEDA: (Celt.) warlike
CEDOMIL: (Slav.) a lover of children
CEDRIC: (Celt.) war chief
CEDRON: (Lat.) cedar tree
CELYNEN: (Wel.) holly
CERI: (Wel.) loved one
CERWYN: (Wel.) fair love
CHAD: (Celt.) martial
CHAIM: (Heb.) life
CHALMERS: (Teut.) a chamberlain
CHANDLER: (Eng.) a merchant; (Lat.-Fr.) a candlemaker
CHAPMAN: (Teut.) merchant
CHARLES: (Teut.) robust; of noble spirit; manly
CHARLIE: a variant of Charles
CHARLTON: (Old Eng.) settlement of free men
CHASE: (Eng.) huntsman
CHAUNCEY: (Teut.) chancellor
CHE: (Span.) diminutive of José
CHELSEA: (Teut.) chalk port
CHENEY: (Lat.) dweller in an oak wood
CHESNEY: (Fr.) an oak grove
CHESTER: (Teut.) urban dweller
CHILWIN: (Gr.) perfect
CHIMA: (Old Eng.) hilly land
CHISHOLM: (Teut.) dweller on gravelled land
CHRIS: diminutives of Christian and Christopher
CHRISTIAN: (Gr.) a follower of Christ's teaching
CHRISTOPHER: (Gr.) Christ-bearer (same as French Christophe, Italian Cristoforo, Spanish Cristobal, German Christoph)
CLARENCE: (Lat.) illustrious, famous

CLARENDON: (Lat.) famous gentleman
CLARIDGE: (Teut.) illustrious
CLARK: (Old Eng.) clergyman; learned man; reader
CLAUD, CLAUDE: English and French forms of Claudius
CLAUDIUS: (Lat.) lame
CLAYTON: (Teut.) from the town on the clay beds
CLEDWYN: (Wel.) blessed sword
CLEMENT: (Lat.) merciful; mild
CLENTON: (Teut.) dweller on the summit
CLEON: (Gr.) glorious
CLEVE: (Teut.) a cleft in the land
CLIFFORD: (Teut.) dweller by the ford by the cliff
CLIFTON: (Eng.) dweller at the manor by the cleft rock
CLINTON: (Ang.-Sax.) from a farm on the headland
CLIVE: origin obscure, but revived from surname of Robert Clive, eighteenth-century soldier and statesman, also title of poem by Browning
CLYDE: (see Clydias)
CLYDIAS: (Gr.) glorious
CODY: (Irish) descendant of a helpful person
COEL: (Wel.) trust
COLA: (Celt.) victorious
COLBERT: (Teut.) cool brightness
COLBRAN: (Teut.) firebrand
COLBURN: (Teut.) dweller by the cold brook
COLE: (Eng.) coal; dark one
COLERIDGE: (Teut.) dweller by the black ridge
COLGAR: (Celt.) proud warrior
COLIN: (Gr.) victory; (Lat.) dove
COLLEY: (Ang.-Sax.) swarthy; black-haired
COLLINS: (Gr.) victorious
COLTON: (Eng.) swarthy
COLUMBUS: (Lat.) dove
COLVIN: (Teut.) dark friend

COMAN: (Arab.) noble
COMPTON: (Lat.) accumulation
CON: (Celt.) wisdom
CONAL(L): (Gael.) daring all
CONAN: (Celt.) high in wisdom
CONNELL: (Celt.) wise chief
CONNOR: (Teut.) an examiner or inspector
CONRAD: (Teut.) bold and wise counsellor
CONROY: (Gael.) hound of the plain
CONSTANT: English form of Constantine
CONSTANTINE: (Lat.) faithful; resolute
CONWAE: (Celt.) strength; vigour
CONWAY: (Celt.) he who takes a wise course
COOPER: (Eng.) barrel-maker
CORBET: (Old Fr.) raven
CORBIN: (Old Fr.) black-haired; raucous
CORDELL: (Lat.) a cord
COREY: (Old Eng.) the chosen
CORMAC: doubtful origin, but probably from (Celt.) son of a charioteer
CORNELIUS: (Lat.) horn-like
CORNELL: (Teut.) a dogwood tree
CORRIE: (Gael.) from the mountains
CORWIN: (Teut.) the heart's friend
COSMO: (Gr.) orderly
COURTENAY, COURTNEY: (Teut.) dweller at the farm; (Fr.) a place name
COVELL: (Old Eng.) wearer of a cowl
COWAN: (Scottish) a stonemason who has not served an apprenticeship
CRAD(D)OCK: (Celt.) beloved; affectionate
CRAIG: (Gael). from the mountain crag
CRAMER: (Teut.) a merchant
CRAWFORD: (Old Eng.) from the crow's ford
CREON: (Old Eng.) accepted doctrine

CRISPIAN, CRISPIN: (Lat.) curled; having curly hair
CRONAN: (Gr.) a mournful tune
CROSBY: (Teut.) dweller by the crossing
CRUZ: (Span.) cross
CULLAN, CULLEN: (Gael.) at the back of the river
CULVER: (Lat.) a dove
CURRAN: (Celt.) hero
CURT, CURTIS: (Fr.) courteous
CURZON: (Teut.) a stump
CUTHBERT: (Teut.) brilliant wisdom; (Ang.-Sax.) famous splendour
CYNAN: (Wel.) chief
CYPRIAN: (Lat.) of Cyprus
CYRIL: (Gr.) lord and master; lordly
CYRO: (Pers.) lordly
CYRUS: (Pers.) throne, near the sun

D

DAEGAL: (Scan.) a son born at dawn
DAFYDD: Welsh variant of David
DAI: (Celt.) to shine
DAIVA: (Irish) a god in Irish mythology
DALBERT: (Teut.) from the bright valley
DALE: (Ang.-Sax.) dweller in a vale between hills
DALLAS: (Celt.) dweller in the field near the waterfall
DALTON: (Ang.-Sax.) dweller in the vale near the village
DALY: (Gael.) assembly
DALZIEL: (Gael.) I dare
DAMIAN: (Gr.) taming
DAMON: English variant of Damian
DAN: (Heb.) judge or law-giver; also contraction of Daniel
DANA: (Celt.) darling
DANIEL: (Heb.) my judge is God; divine judge
DANTE: (Lat.) enduring
DARAH: (Teut.) bold
DARBY: (Celt.) freeman; (Old Eng.) faithful; also Irish contraction of Diarmid or Diarmaid

DARCY, D'ARCY: (Celt.) dark

DARIAN: (Gr.) daring

DARIUS: (Pers.) preserver; he that informs himself

DARNELL: (Old Eng.) hidden brook

DARRELL: (see Daryl)

DARREN: (Eng.) variant form of Daryl

DARSHAN: (Hin.) vision

DARWIN: (Teut.) courageous friend; (Cymric) an oak

DARYL: (Ang.-Sax.) darling

DAVID: (Heb.) beloved friend

DAWSON: (Old Eng.) son of David

DAYTON: (Eng.) David's or Day's settlement

DEACON: (Old Eng.) servant; messenger

DEAN(E): (Teut.) dweller in the valley

DEARBORN: (Teut.) well-born

DECLAN: (Gael.) full of goodness

DEDAN: (Heb.) darling; Abraham's kin

DEDWYDD: (Wel.) happy

DELANEY: (Gael.-Old Fr.) dark challenger; from the elder grove

DELANO: (Gael.) healthy, dark man; (Lat.-Fr.) alder grove

DELBERT: (Teut.) nobly bright

DELMAR: (Lat.) man of the sea

DELWIN: (Teut.) godly friend

DEMAS: (Lat.) respected

DEMETRIUS: (Gr.) harvest-lover

DEMPSEY: (Celt.) proud

DEMPSTER: (Old Eng.) wise as a judge

DENHAM: (Ang.-Sax.) from a home in the valley

DENHOLM: (Old Eng.) island valley

DENIS, DENNIS: (Gr.) of Dionysius; name frequently used in Ireland, and from which Dennison, Denny, and Dennys are derived

DENMAN: (Ang.-Sax.) a man of the valley

DENTON: (Old Eng.) settlement in the valley
DEON: (Gr.) of Zeus
DERBY: (Ang.-Sax.) the place of the deer
DEREK, DERRICK: (Teut.) people's ruler; Dutch form Diederich, and Old German form Theodoric
DERMOT: (Celt.) father of oaks; an Irish contraction of Diarmid or Diarmaid
DERWENT: origin unknown; a river name in England
DERWIN: (Ang.-Sax.) valued friend of the people
DERWOOD: (Teut.) door warden
DESMO: (Gr.) a chain
DESMOND: (Celt.) man of the world
DEVANEY: (Celt.) black strife
DEVARA: (Sans.) husband or lover
DEVEREAUX: (Old Fr.) dutiful
DEVLIN: (Celt.) heroic; (Gael.) a pilgrim
DEWAR: (Gael.) a pilgrim; (Celt.) heroic
DEXTER: (Lat.) skilful
DICK: contraction of Richard
DIDIER: (Fr.) greatly desired
DIEGO: (Heb.) supplanter
DIETER: (Teut.) warrior race
DIGBY: (Teut.) a digger
DIGGORY: (Fr.) strayed; lost
DILLON: (Celt.) faithful
DILWYN: (Teut.) calm friend
DINO: variant form of Dean
DINSMORE: (Teut.) the great fort
DION: (Gr.) divine
DIONYSIUS: (see Denis)
DIXON: (Eng.) son of Richard
DOANE: (Celt.) a song
DOLAN: (Celt.) black-haired
DOMINGO: (Span.) Sunday child
DOMINIC: (Lat.) of the Lord; born on a Sunday

DON: (Lat.) master; diminutive of Donald
DONAGHAN: (Celt.) of dark complexion
DONAHUE: (Celt.) dark
DONALD: (Celt.) proud or mighty chief
DONATO: (Lat.) a gift
DONNELLY: (Celt.) brave, dark man
DONOVAN: (Celt.) dark warrior
DORAN: (Gael.) a stranger
DORIAN: (Gr.) a gift
DORMAN: (Lat.) a sleeper
DORMAND: (Teut.) beloved protector
DOUGAL: (Celt.) dark stranger
DOUGLAS: (Gael.) dark river
DOVEL: (Teut.) a young dove
DOYLE: (Celt.) dark stranger
DRACO: (Lat.) dragon
DRAKE: (Eng.) dragon
DREW: (Teut.) skilful; diminituve of Andrew
DRISCOLL: (Teut.) a thicket of wild roses
DRUMMOND: (Celt.) dweller on the hill
DUAN(E): (Celt.) a poem or song
DUBERT: (Teut.) bright knight
DUDLEY: a surname derived from Dudley in Worcestershire and made famous by the Dudley family that rose to power under the Tudors
DUDON: (Lat.) God-given
DUFF: (Gael.) dark-haired
DUKE: (Lat.) a leader
DUNBAR: (Celt.) dark branch
DUNCAN: (Celt.) dark or brown chief
DUNLEA: (Teut.) from the dark meadow
DUNSTAN: (Teut.) of lofty station; (Old Eng.) compound of hill and stone
DURAND: (Lat.) enduring, lasting
DURANT: (Lat.) endurance
DURHAM: (Teut.) dweller on a hilly island

DURWIN: (Ang.-Sax.) dear friend
DURWOOD: (Teut.) unflinching guard
DUSTIN: (Teut.) a fighter
DWIGHT: origin obscure, perhaps derived from Diot, a diminutive of Dionisia
DWYER: (Gael.) dark wise one
DYER: (Old Eng.) a colourer of skin and fabrics
DYFAN: (Wel.) tribe ruler
DYFRIG: (Wel.) princely hero
DYLAN: (Wel.) creative; from the sea
DYNAMI: (N.A. Ind.) an eagle
DYNAND: (Cymric) given

E

EAGAN, EGAN: (Irish) spirited
EAMON: (Irish) variant form of Edmond – rich protection
EARL, EARLE: (Teut.) of keen intelligence
EARN: (Teut.) an eagle
EATON: (Ang.-Sax.) from the riverside
EBEN: (Heb.) stone; a diminutive of Ebenezer
EBENEZER: (Heb.) stone of help
EBER: (Heb.) one that passes
EBERARD: (Teut.) strong and hardy
EBERT: (Fr.) bright; (Teut.) of active mind
ECTOR: (Slav.) dedicated
ED: (Teut.) wealth; (Heb.) a witness; also a diminutive of Edward
EDAN: (Celt.) fire
EDBERT: (Ang.-Sax.) rich and generous
EDDY: (Scan.) unresting
EDEL: (Teut.) noble
EDEN: (Heb.) delight
EDGAR: (Teut.) rich spear; (Ang.-Sax.) dart
EDISON: (Eng.) son of Edward
EDLIN, EDLUN: (Teut.-Ang.-Sax.) a nobleman

of a prosperous village
EDMEAD: (Ang.-Sax.) noble reward
EDMOND, EDMUND: (Teut.) rich protection; (Ang.-Sax.) defender of property
EDRED: (Teut.) rich counsel
EDRIC: (Teut.) rich ruler
EDSEL: (Teut.) rich in self
EDWALD: (Teut.) rich in power
EDWARD: (Teut.) rich ward, guardian of property
EDWIN: (Teut.) rich friend
EFRAIN: (Heb.) fruitful
EGA: (Teut.) formidable
EGAN: (Gael.) strong-handed
EGBERT: (Teut.) eminently bright; (Ang.-Sax.) skilled with the sword
EGMONT: (Ang.-Sax.) sword protection; (Teut.) powerful protector; a famous Flemish patriot
EINAR: (Scan.) warrior chief; (Gr.) one who is sent
EIROS: (Wel.) bright
ELAM: (Heb.) eternal
ELBERT: (see Albert)
ELDO: (Gr.) a wish
ELDON: (Lat.) the gift
ELDORIS: (Teut.) spear-point
ELDRED: (Teut.) mature counsellor
ELDWIN: (Teut.) old friend
ELEAZAR: (Heb.) God helped
ELFED: (Wel.) autumn
ELFORD: (Teut.) dweller by the ford
ELGIN: (Gael.) earldom of the Bruces of Scotland
ELI: (Heb.) elevation; the high
ELIA: (Heb.) God's own
ELIAN: (Lat.) brilliant
ELIAS: (Lat.) cheerful
ELIJAH: (Heb.) my God is the Lord
ELIK: (Haw.) powerful leader
ELIKA: (Heb.) purified by God
ELIOT, ELLIOT, ELLIOTT: (Heb.) God's own given one

ELISHA: (Heb.) God is generous; God is my salvation
ELKAN: (Heb.) God created
ELKI: (N.A. Ind.) bear
ELLERT: (Old Fr.) God's own gift
ELLERY: (Old Eng.) elder tree
ELLIS: English variant of Elisha
ELMEN: (Teut.) sturdy like an oak tree
ELMER: (Ang.-Sax.) noble
ELMO: (Gr.) amiable
ELMORE: (Teut.) the greater
ELON: (Heb.) the sturdy oak
ELRED: (Ang.-Sax.) noble counsel
ELROD: (Teut.) celebrated
ELROY: (Lat.) regal
ELTON: (Old Eng.) Ella's settlement
ELVAN: (Teut.) quick-willed
ELVERT: (Lat.) variable
ELVIS: (Scan.) all-wise
ELWIN, ELWYN: Godly friend
ELWOOD: (Teut.) forest-dweller
EMANUEL, EMMANUEL: (Heb.) God (is) with us
EMERIA: (Teut.) industrious worker
EMERSON: (Eng.) son of Emery
EMERY: (Teut.) powerful; (Ang.-Sax.) strong; rich
EMIL: (Teut.) industrious
EMILIO: (It.) competitive; (Span.) excelling
EMMET(T): (Lat.) industrious
EMO: (Teut.) serious; also possibly derived from the Irish surname Emagh
EMRE: (Turk.) fraternal bond
EMRYS: a Welsh name derived from Ambrose
EMYR: (Wel.) honour
ENAN: (Wel.) anvil; firm
ENEAS: (Gr.) worthy of praise
ENGELBERT: (Teut.) bright messenger
ENNIS: (Gr.) from Ennea; nine
ENOCH: (Heb.) the dedicated

ENOLD: (Teut.) the anointed
ENOS: (Heb.) man, mortal
ENSLEY: (Celt.) a watchword
ENZO: (It.) giant
EOGHAN: (Celt.) young warrior
EPHRAIM: (Heb.) fruitful
ERASMUS: (Gr.) the desired
ERASTUS: (Gr.) amiable
ERBERT: (Teut.) always alert
ERHARD: (Teut.) intelligent resolution
ERIC: (Teut.) kingly; (Ang.-Sax.) brave; powerful
ERLAND: (Teut.) foreign, from a foreign land
ERLON: (Teut.) elfish
ERMIN: (Cymric) lordly
ERMOS: (Teut.) popular
ERNEST: (Teut.) of serious purpose
ERNST: German form of Ernest
ERROL: (Lat.) wandering
ERSKINE: (Scottish) high cliff
ERVAND: (Scan.) sea warrior
ERWIN: (Teut.) friend
ESAU: (Heb.) he that finishes; also, rough, hairy
ESBERN: (Teut.) divine leader
ESDRAS: (Heb.) a rising light
ESME: a Scottish use of the French Esme, which is derived from the Latin, meaning esteemed
ESMOND: (Teut.) protected by the gods
ESTEVAN: (Basque-Gr.) a crown
ETAM: (Lat.) of the warrior's house
ETENIA: (N.A. Ind.) wealthy
ETHAN: (Heb.) firmness
ETHELBERT: (Ang.-Sax.) noble and bright
ETHELRED: (Ang.-Sax.) noble strength; noble counsel
ETU: (N.A. Ind.) the sun
EUBULE: (Gr.) good counsellor
EUCLID: (Gr.) true glory
EUCRATES; (Gr.) good-tempered

EUDON: (Gr.-Teut.) rich master

EUDORA: (Gr.) generous

EUGENE: (Gr.) well-born, noble

EURWYN: (Wel.) golden fair

EUSEBIUS: (Gr.) pious; God-fearing

EUSTACE: (Gr.) fruitful harvest; steadfast

EVAN: (Celt.) young warrior

EVAR: (Heb.) life

EVERARD: (Teut.) ever courageous; strong as a boar

EVERETT: (Teut.) courageous

EWALD: (Teut.) always powerful

EWAN, EWEN: (Celt.) warrior

EWART: (Teut.) brave

EWING: (Eng.) law friend

EYMER: (Teut.) royal toiler

EZAR: (Heb.) treasure

EZEKIEL: (Heb.) may God strengthen

EZRA: (Heb.) help, the helpful

F

FABIAN: (Lat.) thought to have derived from 'faba', a bean, therefore a bean-grower; other authorities give this as dilatory

FABIO: (It.) seductive; handsome

FABRON: (Lat.) a man who works with his hands

FADIL: (Arab.) giving

FAGAN: (Celt.) small voice

FAIRBURN: (Teut.) comely child

FAIRCHILD: (Teut.) blond child

FAIRFAX: (Teut.) fair-haired

FAIRHOLD: (Teut.) powerful

FAISAL: (Arab.) judge; resolute

FALKNER: (Teut.) trainer of hawks

FANE: (Teut.) joyful

FARAMOND: (Teut.) travel protection

FARAND: (Teut.) attractive
FARLEY: (Teut.) unexpected
FARMAN: (Teut.) traveller
FARNHAM: (Teut.) village in the ferns
FAROUK: (Arab.) one who can tell right from wrong
FARQUHAR: (Gael.) friendly man
FARRAR: (Fr.) distinguished
FARREL: (Arab.) a bearer of burdens
FAULKNER: (Lat.) falcon
FAUSTINO: (Lat.) fortunate
FAXON: (Teut.) long-haired
FEARGAL, FERGAL: (Gael.) man of valour
FEICHIN: (Gael.) raven
FELIM: (Celt.) constantly good
FELIX: (Lat.) happy
FENNER: (Teut.) from the lowlands
FENTON: (Old Eng.) settlement on the marsh
FENWICK: (Teut.) from the marshland
FENWOOD: (Teut.) dweller in the lowlands forest
FEODORE: a variant of Theodore
FERDINAND: (Teut.) venturing; brave
FERENC: (Hung.) free
FERGUS: (Celt.) man strength
FERMIN: (Lat.) steadfast
FERNER: (Teut.) distant
FERRER: (Span.) blacksmith
FERRIS: (Lat.) man of iron
FESTUS: (Lat.) the joyful
FIDEL: (Lat.) faithful
FILIBERT: (Teut.) of flashing will
FILMER: (Teut.) most famous
FINBAR: (Gael.) fair-headed
FINDAL: (Teut.) inventive
FINDLAY: (Teut.) capable
FINGAL: (Celt.) a mythical Irish hero; white stranger
FINLAY: (Gael.) fair warrior
FINLEY: (Gael.) sunbeam
FINNEGAN: (Celt.) fair
FITZGERALD: (Eng.) son of Gerald
FLAVIAN: (Lat.) yellow-haired

FLEMING: (Eng.) man from Flanders
FLETCHER: (Teut.) arrow-maker
FLINN, FLYNN: (Gael.) son of the red-haired one
FLO: (N.A. Ind.) arrow-like
FLOBERT: (Teut.) of glorious fame
FLOREAN, FLORIAN: (Lat.) flower beauty
FLOYD: (Wel.) grey-haired
FORD: (Teut.) crossing or passing
FORTESCUE: (Teut.-Fr.) strong shield
FOSTER: (Old Eng.) a forester
FOTINI: (Gr.) light
FRANCIS: (Teut.) free
FRANK: an English contraction of Francis
FRANKLIN, FRANKLYN: (Teut.) a freeman
FRASER: (Scottish) of the forest men
FRAYNE: (Teut.) the ash tree
FRED, FREDDIE: English contractions of Frederick
FREDERICK: (Teut.) peace ruler
FREEMAN: (Ang.-Sax.) not a slave
FREWEN: (Ang.-Sax.) free friend
FRITH: (Ang.-Sax.) dweller in the woodland
FRITZ: (Teut.) peaceful ruler
FRYSA: (Frie.) curly-haired
FULBERT: (Teut.) bright, shining
FULVIAN, FULVIUS: (Lat.) tawny

G

GABINO: (Lat.) God is my strength
GABRIEL: (Heb.) strong man of God
GAD: (Heb.) lucky; audacious
GADMAN(N): (Heb.) the fortunate one
GAGE: (Fr.) dedicated
GAIUS: (Lat.) joyful
GALAHAD: (Celt.) valorous; name of spotless knight who succeeded in his quest for the Holy Grail

GALE: (Scan.) a wind; (Dan.) a crow

GALEN: (Gr.) healer; probably named after the second-century Greek physician

GALILEO: (It.) man from Galilee

GALLAGHER: (Gael.) foreign helper

GALLOWAY: (Gael.) stranger

GALPIN: (Old Fr.) a runner

GALVIN: (Celt.) sparrow

GANESH: (Hin.) lord of the throngs; a Hindu deity

GANYA: (Rus.) strong

GARALT: (Teut.) brave warrior

GARCIA: (Teut.) a warrior

GARDELL(E): (Teut.) a careful guard

GARETH: (Wel.) gentle

GARFIELD: (Teut.) spear field

GARLAND: (Eng.-Fr.) crown; wreath

GARNER, GARNIER: (Teut.) protecting warrior

GARNET, GARRET: (Teut.) strong with the spear

GAROLD: (Teut.) powerful warrior

GARRICK: (Teut.) warrior king

GARRY: (see Garvey)

GARTH: (Ang.-Sax.) form of gardener

GARVEY: (Teut.) spear-bearer

GARVIN: (Teut.) warrior-friend

GASPARD: (Pers.) treasure-master

GASTON: (Teut.) hospitable; (Span.) beautiful town

GAVIN: (Celt.) hawk of battle

GAWAIN: a Welsh form of Gavin

GAYLE: (Teut.) a jailor

GAYLORD: (Teut.) merry lord

GAYNELL: (Teut.) one who profits

GAYNOR: (Celt.) fair head

GEBHARD: (Teut.) determined giver

GELBERT: (Teut.) bright pledge

GEMMEL: (Scan.) old
GENE: a contraction of Eugene
GENESIUS: (Lat.) welcome newcomer
GENTILIS: (Lat.) the kind one
GEOFFREY: (Teut.-Fr.) God's peace
GEORGE: (Gr.) tiller of the soil
GERAINT: (Teut.) unerring spear
GERALD: (Teut.) strong with a spear
GERARD: English form of Gerald
GERHARD: German form of Gerard
GERIUS: (Lat.) steadfast; constant
GERONIMO: (It.) sacred name
GERRY: diminutive of Gerald and Gerard
GERSHAM, GERSHOM: (Heb.) exiled
GERT: (Teut.) strong spear
GERVAISE: (Teut.) alert warrior
GERWYN: (Wel.) fair love
GETHIN: (Wel.) dark of skin
GIACOMO: (It.) God's son
GIBSON: (Eng.) smiling
GIDEON: (Heb.) a hewer
GIFFORD: (Teut.) a passing
GILBERT: (Teut.) bright pledge
GILCHRIST: (Celt.) servant of Christ
GILDAS: (Lat.-Gael.) servant of God
GILES: (Gr.) a shield, or shield-bearer; (Lat.) a young goat
GILFORD: (Teut.) dweller by the big ford
GILLAND: (Teut.) bold youth
GILLES: (Fr.) miraculous
GILLIAN: (Celt.) servant of the saints
GILMAN: (Teut.) big man
GILMORE, GILMOUR: (Teut.) big servant; (Celt.) a servant of Mary
GINO: (It.) well-born
GLADE: (Old Eng.) shining
GLADSTONE: (Ang.-Sax.) polished rock

GLADWIN: (Teut.) merry friend
GLANMOR: (Wel.) seashore
GLANVILLE: (Old Eng.) clean field
GLEN: (Teut.) a dale
GLEVE: (Teut.) point of a spear
GLOVER: (Teut.) one who makes or sells gloves
GLYNN: (Teut.) from the glen
GODDARD: (Teut.) divinely resolute; pious
GODFREY: (Teut.) peace of God
GODRIC: (Teut.) friend of God
GODWIN: (Ang.-Sax.) brave in war
GOLDWIN, GOLDWYN: (Ang.-Sax.) gold-friend
GOMER: (Heb.) complete
GOMEZ: (Span.-Teut.) man
GORDON: (Teut.) dweller at the triangular hill estate
GORHAM: (Old Eng.) dweller at the mud house
GORMAN: (Teut.) man of clay
GOVERT: (Gr.) control
GRADY: (Irish) noble; hardworking
GRAHAM: (Teut.) dweller in the grey manor; stern
GRANT: (Old Eng.) a promise
GRANTHAM: (Old Eng.) a home acquired by deed
GRANVILLE: (Old Fr.) from the big city
GRASHAM, GRESHAM: (Teut.) dweller on the grassland
GRATTAN: (Teut.) an enclosure
GREGG: (Teut.) increase
GREGORY: (Gr.) watchful
GRIFFITH: (Lat.) ruddy
GRIMBALD: (Old Fr.) a bold son
GRISWOLD: (Teut.) from the wild forest
GROSVENOR: (Old Fr.) great hunter
GROVER: (Teut.) one who dwells among the trees
GRUFFYDD: (Wel.) strong warrior
GRUGWYN: (Wel.) white heather

GUIDO: (Teut.) a guide
GUILFORD: (Teut.) William's ford
GUILLYM: a Welsh form of William
GULLIVER: (Eng.) glutton
GUNTHAR: (Teut.) warrior; bold
GURIAS: (Heb.) of a nomadic family
GURTH: (Teut.) bonded
GUSTAV(E), GUSTAVUS: (Teut.) Goth's staff
GUTHRIE: (Celt.) war hero; (Ang.-Sax.) wise rule
GUY: (Celt.) sensible; (Fr.) guide, leader
GWERN: (Wel.) the alder tree
GWION: (Wel.) elf
GWYN: (Cymric) a hunter
GWYNFOR: (Wel.) a fair place

H

HAAKON: (Scan.) of high race
HABIB: (Syriac) beloved
HABOR: (Teut.) dexterous
HACHMANN: (Heb.) a learned man
HADAR: (Heb.) respected
HADDEN: (Old Eng.) of the moors
HADLEY: (Teut.) landholder
HADRIAN: a variant form of Adrian
HADWIN: (Ang.-Sax.) family friend
HAFIZ: (Arab.) one who remembers
HAGAR: (Heb.) wanderer
HAGBERT: (Teut.) skilful
HAIM: (Heb.) alive
HAIMA: (Sans.) made of gold
HAINES: (Cymric) one who helps himself
HAKAN: (N.A. Ind.) fiery
HAKEEM: (Arab.) wise; insightful
HAKON: (Scan.) chosen son
HAL: (Ang.-Sax.) healthy; (Teut.) in sound health; also a contraction of Henry or Harold
HALBERT: (see Albert)

HALDANE, HALDEN: (Ang.-Sax.-Scan.) half-Dane
HALL: (Teut.) stone or rock; a manor house
HALLAM: (Teut.) a threshold
HALLETT: (Teut.) dweller at the little manor
HALLWORTH: (Old Nor.) an amulet
HALMAR: (Scan.) helmet glory
HALSEY: (Eng.) isolated
HAMAL: (Turk.) a carrier
HAMAN: (Heb.) magnificent
HAMBLIN: (Teut.) crippled
HAMFORD: (Teut.) from the black ford
HAMID: (Arab.) praiseworthy
HAMISH: Gaelic form of James
HAMLYN: (Teut.) home-lover
HAMO: (Teut.) home
HAMON: (Gr.) faithful
HAN: (Scan.) the Lord is gracious
HANEEF: (Arab.) believer
HANK: (Teut.) home ruler; also a form of Henry
HANLEY: (Teut.-Ang.-Sax.) of the meadowland
HANNIBAL: (Pho.) grace of the supreme being; (Egyp.) favoured of Baal
HANNO: (Pho.) grace
HANS: a German form of John
HANSEL: (Heb.) God's grace
HARALD: a Danish form of Harold
HARDING: (Teut.) resolute
HAREM: (Heb.) a mountaineer
HARI: (Sans.) yellow-brown
HARIM: (Heb.) flat-nosed
HARLAN(D): (Teut.) battle country
HARLEY: (Teut.) deer-hunter
HAROLD: (Teut.) a compound of 'here' and 'weald' – army and power; (Ang.-Sax.) a champion; a general
HAROWIN: (Teut.) hard friend
HARPER: (Teut.) harp player

HARRISON: (Eng.) son of Harry
HARRY: English form of Henry
HART: (Teut.) the stag
HARTLEY: (Teut.) dweller by the lea of the stags
HARTMAN: (Teut.) the firm one
HARVEY: (Celt.) progressive
HASAKA: (Sans.) a jester
HASIN: (Sans.) laughter, laughing
HASSAN: (Arab.) handsome
HASTINGS: (Teut.) swift
HAVELOCK: (Lat.) tent
HAVILAH: (Heb.) plentiful of treasure
HAYDEN: (Teut.) dweller on a ledged hill
HAYES: modern usage
HAYMON: an Old English variant of Hamo
HAYWARD: (Teut.) guard of the ledge
HAYWOOD: (Teut.) the wood within the ledge
HAZEN: (Teut.) a hare
HEATH: (Teut.) a high plain
HEATHCOAT, HEATHCOTT: (Ang.-Sax.) cottage on the heath
HEBER: (Heb.) partner
HEBERT: (Teut.) man of brilliance
HECTOR: (Gr.) an anchor; thought to have originally meant holding fast
HEDLEY: (Teut.) the upper meadow
HEILYN: (Wel.) cup-bearer
HEINRICH: a German form of Henry
HELBERT: (Teut.) bright healer
HELGA: (Nor.) holy
HELIOS: (Gr.) sun
HENDRY: (Teut.) manly
HENDY: (Teut.) skilful
HENLY: (Teut.) home lover
HENRY: (Teut.) ruler of the home
HER(R)IOT: obsolete diminutive of Henry
HERBERT: (Teut.) bright warrior; (Ang.-Sax.) army hero
HERMAN: (Teut.) army or war man

HERMES: (Gr.) messenger
HERRICK: (Teut.) army commander
HERVEY: (Celt.) progressive
HEW: (Celt.) mind; a variant of Hugh
HEYWARD: (Teut.) dweller by the dark forest
HEZEKIAH: (Heb.) God is strength
HIDEKI: (Jap.) excellent trees
HILARY: (Lat.) cheerful
HILDER: (Teut.) fighting man
HILLEL: (Heb.) greatly praised
HILLIARD: (Teut.) war guardian
HILTON: (Old Eng.) from the house on the hill
HINMAN: (Teut.) one who saves
HIRAM: (Heb.) nobly born
HIRO: (Span.) sacred name
HIROSHI: (Jap.) generous
HOBART: a variant of Hubert
HODGE: (Teut.) famous swordsman
HOGAN: (Dutch) eminent
HOLDEN: (Teut.) gracious; kind
HOLMAN(N): (Dutch) man of the hollow; (Teut.) from the river island
HOMER: (Gr.) pledge; (Ang.-Sax.) pool in a hollow
HORACE, HORATIO: (Lat.) light of the sun; worthy
HOSEA: (Heb.) salvation; also related to Joshua
HOUGHTON: (Teut.) dweller at the hill estate
HOUSTON: (Ang.-Sax) from a hill town
HOWARD: (Teut.) hedge guard
HOWELL: (Wel.) eminent
HOWLAND: (Old Eng.) of the hills
HOYT: (Nor.) spirit; soul
HUBBARD: (Teut.) intellectual
HUBERT: (Teut.) bright
HUGH: (Teut.) intellectual
HUGO: a form of Hugh
HULBERT: (Teut.) bright; faithful

HUMBERT: (Teut.) bright giant
HUME: (Teut.) home-lover
HUMPHREY: (Ang.-Sax.) protector of the home
HUNTER: (Teut.) huntsman
HURLEY: Irish game of hockey
HUXLEY: (Old Eng.) Hugh's meadow
HUYA: (N.A. Ind.) fighting eagle
HYLAND: (Teut.) highlander
HYMAN: (Teut.) high dweller
HYWEL: (Wel.) eminent

I

IA(I)N: (see John)
IAGO: (Heb.) supplanter
IAN: (Heb.) God's grace
IBALD: (Teut.) princely archer
IBRAHIM: (Arab.) father of many
IBU: (Jap.) creative
ICABOD: (Heb.) departed glory
ICHIRO: (Jap.) first-born son
IDDEN: (Ang.-Sax) a prosperous man
IDDO: (Heb.) loving
IDRIS: (Wel.) driven by impulse
IESTIN, IESTYN: (Wel.) the just; from the Latin 'iustus'
IEUAN: a Welsh form of John
IFOR: a Welsh form of Ivor
IGNATIUS: (Lat.) ardent; (Gr.) the kindled flame
IGOR: (Scan.) hero
IKAIKA: (Haw.) strong
IKE: (Heb.) variant form of Isaac
ILBERT: (Teut.) strife
ILLAH: (Heb.) a tree
ILLARIS: (Gr.) merry
ILLTYD: (Wel.) ruler of a town or district
IMALA: (N.A. Ind.) a disciplinarian
IMMANUEL: (see Emanuel)
IMO: (Gr.) beloved
IMRAN: (Arab.) host
INDIANA: (Lat.) from India

INDRA: (Hin.) lord of the sky gods
INGMAR: (Scan.) famous son
INGOMA: (Teut.) of Ing's fame
INGRAM: (Teut.) raven
INIGO: origin obscure; name of a bishop of Antioch, martyred between AD104 and 117; also name of English architect, Inigo Jones
INIR: (Wel.) honour
INNIS: (Teut.) sheltered valley
IOAN: (Slav.) believer
IONWYN: (Wel.) fair lord
IRA: (Heb.) descendant; (Aramaic) the stallion
IRAM: (Heb.) citizen
IRFON: (Wel.) the anointed one
IRVING: (Eng.) attractive
IRWIN: (Eng.) practical
ISA: (Gr.) equal
ISAAC: (Heb.) laughter
ISADORE: (Gr.) gift of Isis
ISAIAH: (Heb.) the Lord is his salvation
ISAM: (Arab.) protector
ISARD: (Teut.) inflexible as iron
ISAS: (Jap.) meritorious
ISHI: (Heb.) husband
ISHMAEL: (Heb.) God heareth
ISIDORE: (Gr.) gift of Isis
ISMAN: (Heb.) faithful husband
ISRAEL: (Heb.) authorities give this as both 'may God prevail' and 'soldier of God'
ITHEL: (Wel.) generous lord
ITHNAN: (Heb.) the strong sailor
IVAN: Russian form of John
IVANDER: (Heb.) divine man
IVER: (Old Scan.) military archer
IVOR: (Teut.) bow bearer
IXARA: (Sans.) master; prince
IZOD: (Celt.) fair

J

JABEZ: (Heb.) obscure meaning, but some

authorities give it as sorrow
JABIN: (Heb.) born of God
JABIR: (Arab.) supportive
JABRIEL: (Heb.) God-health
JACE: (Heb.) healer
JACK: an English contraction of John; nineteenth-century authority stated that, contrary to belief at the time, there was no confirmation of the theory that Jack or Jakke was ever used to represent Jacques or James
JACKSON: (Eng.) son of Jack
JACOB: (Heb.) a supplanter
JACQUES: French form of James
JADA: (Sans.) frigid
JADDA: (Heb.) man of wisdom
JADEN: (Heb.) Jehovah has heard
JAFAR: (Arab.) stream
JAGO: (Eng.) self-assured
JAHAN: (Sans.) worldly
JAHIR: (Hin.) jewel
JAHMAL: (Arab.) beautiful
JAIR, JAIRUS: (Heb.) enlightened by God
JAKE: (Heb.) supplanter
JAKEH: (Heb.) pious
JALAL: (Hin.) glory
JAMES: from Jacobus; English form of Jacob
JAMIE: (Heb.) supplanter; a variant of James
JAN: a dialectal form of John
JANITRA: (Sans.) of high origin
JANUS: (Lat.) opener; sometimes given as two-faced, relating to the two-faced god of doors
JAPHET(H): (Heb.) may he expand
JARED: (Gr.) rose
JARIUS: (Span.) generous
JARRATT: (Teut.) firm combatant
JARVIS: (Old Eng.) a driver
JASON: (Gr.) healer
JASPER: (Pers.) treasure-seeker
JAVAS: (Sans.) swift
JAVIER: (Span.) bright

JAY: (Teut.) gay
JAYDEN: modern usage, meaning bright-eyed
JEAN: French form of John
JEB: (Heb.) jolly
JED: (Heb.) helpful
JEDIDIAH: (Heb.) beloved of the lord
JEFFERSON: (Teut.) son of peace
JEFFREY: (see Geoffrey)
JEHIAN: (Heb.) his life is Jehovah's
JEHOSHAPHAT: (Heb.) the Lord judges
JEHU: (Heb.) Jehovah is he
JENSON: (Eng.) blessed; son of Jen
JEPHTHAH: (Heb.) God sets free
JEPHUM: (Heb.) he is prepared
JEREMIAH, JEREMY: (Heb.) exalted of God
JERICHO: (Arab.) city of the moon
JERMAINE: (Lat.) brotherly
JERMYN: (Teut.) bright
JEROME: (Gr.) sacred name
JERRY: diminutives of Gerald, Gerard and Jeremy
JERVIS: (Teut.) alert warrior (another form of Gervaise)
JERVOISE: a variant form of Jervis and Gervaise
JERWAIS: (Teut.) armed for battle
JESSE: (Heb.) wealthy
JESUS: (Heb.) saviour; healing
JETHRO: (Heb.) abundance
JEVON: Welsh form of Evan
JIM: an English contraction of James
JIN: (Chin.) golden
JIVANTA: (Sans.) long-lived
JIVIN: (Sans.) vivifying
JOAB: (Heb.) God (Jehovah) is (his) father
JOACHIM: (Heb.) may Jehovah exalt
JOB: (Heb.) persecuted
JOBY: (Heb.) patient; tested
JOCELIN: (Lat.) sportive
JOCK: (see Jacob); also a Scottish form of John
JODA: (Lat.) playful
JODY: (Heb.) believer in Jehovah

JOE: an English contraction of Joseph

JOEL: (Heb.) Jehovah is God

JOHN: (Heb.) Jehovah has favoured; the Lord graciously giveth

JOLON: (N.A. Ind.) valley of the dead oaks

JONAH, JONAS: (Heb.) a dove

JONATHAN: (Heb.) the Lord's gift

JORAH: (Heb.) autumn rain

JORAM: (Heb.) the Lord is exalted

JORDAN: (Heb.) flowing down; descendant

JOSÉ: (Heb.) he will enlarge

JOSEPH: (Heb.) may Jehovah add

JOSHUA: (Heb.) the Lord is salvation; Jehovah is generous

JOSIAH: (Heb.) may Jehovah heal

JOSIAS: a Greek form of Josiah

JOTHAM: (Heb.) Jehovah is perfect

JOVIAN: (Lat.) of Jupiter

JOVITA: (Teut.) little dove

JOYCE: (Lat.) merry; used for both men and women

JUAN: a Spanish form of John

JUBALUS: (Lat.) lute-player

JUDAH: (Heb.) praised

JUDE: (Lat.) form of Judas, meaning praised

JULES: a variant of Julius

JULIAN: a variant of Julius

JULIUS: (Lat.) soft-haired, downy-bearded

JUNIOR: (Lat.) the younger one

JUNIUS: (Lat.) born in June

JURGEN: (Gr.) farmer

JURISA: (Slav.) storm

JUSTIN: (see Justus)

JUSTUS: (Lat.) just; righteous

K

KADEEM: (Arab.) one who serves

KAHLIL: (Arab.) friend

KAI: (Pers.) king

KAINE: (Irish) handsome

KALANI: (Haw.) sky

KALEN: (Gael.) uncertain
KALEVA: (Finn.) a hero
KALO: (Gr.) royal
KALON: (Gr.) noble
KAMAL: (Arab.) perfection; (Sans.) pale red
KAMPER: (Teut.) fighter
KANE: (Lat.) exacted tribute
KAREEM: (Arab.) generous
KARIF: (Arab.) born in Autumn
KARL: (Teut.) a man; German form of Charles
KASPAR: (Pers.) treasure-master
KAY: (Gr.) rejoicing
KEAGAN, KEEGAN: (Gael.) small flame
KEANE: (Celt.) great, vast
KEANU: (Haw.) cool breeze from the mountains
KEARNEY: (Celt.) a soldier
KEATON: (Eng.) place of hawks
KEDAR: (Heb.) dark
KEELER: (Gael.) beautiful; graceful
KEENAN: (Celt.) sharp
KEIR: (Gael.) swarthy
KEIRA: (Teut.) ever-regal
KEITH: (Gael.) the wind
KELBY: (Teut.) from a farm
KELLEN: (Irish) strong-willed
KELLY: (Celt.) a warrior
KELSEY: (Teut.) from the water
KELVIN, KELWIN: (Celt.) dweller by the water
KEMBLE: (Ang.-Sax.) royally bold
KENAZ: (Heb.) hunter
KENDALL: (Celt.) chief of the dale
KENDRICK, KENRICK: (Teut.) distinguished (or royal) ruler
KENELM: (Celt.) beloved chief
KENNA: (Celt.) quick love
KENNEDY: (Celt.) chief of the clan
KENNETH: (Gael.) leader
KENNY: a diminutive of Kenneth
KENSELL: (Teut.) royally brave
KENT: (Celt.) chief
KENWARD: (Teut.) keen guardian

KENWAY: (Ang.-Sax.) valiant soldier
KENWOOD: (Celt.) wooded dell
KENYON: (Celt.) fair-haired
KENZO: (Jap.) wise
KEON: (Haw.) gracious
KERMIT: (Gael.) without envy
KERR: (Celt.) a meadow
KERRIN, KERRYN: variants of Kieren
KERRY: (Ang.-Sax.) captain
KERSEY: (Old Eng.) homely
KERWIN: (Teut.) loving friend
KERWOOD: (Gael.) dweller at the wood by the meadow
KESTER: a variant of Christopher
KETURAH: (Heb.) fragrance
KEVIN: (Celt.) comely; comely birth
KHALID: (Arab.) eternal
KIAN: (Gael.) ancient
KIEFER: (German) barrel-maker
KIERAN, KIEREN: (Celt.) black
KILBURN: (Teut.) keen guardian
KILIAN: (Celt.) the innocent one
KIM: (Ang.-Sax.) chief
KIMBALL: modern usage
KING: (Teut.) chief
KINGSLEY: (Teut.) dweller in the royal meadow
KINGSTON: (Teut.) dweller at the royal residence
KINMAN: (Ang.-Sax.) man of royal blood
KIRBY: (Arab.) a waterskin; (Teut.) from the church village; (Eng.) English place name
KIRK: (Gael.) a house of worship
KIRKHAM: (Teut.) dweller at the church manor
KIRKLAND: (Teut.) dweller on church land
KIRKWOOD: (Teut.) dweller in the wood by the church
KIRLEY: (Arab.) a waterskin

KIT: a contraction of Christopher
KITTO: a pet form of Christopher
KNOWLES: (Teut.) a grassy slope in the forest
KOLBY: (Nor.) settlement
KONRAD: (see Conrad)
KRAMER: (Teut.) shopkeeper
KRISHNA: (Sans.) black
KURTZ: (Teut.) short, laconic in speech
KYLE: (Gael.) a channel or firth
KYNAN: (Celt.) a form of Conal – daring all
KYNE: (Ang.-Sax.) bold
KYRLE: modern usage

L

LABAN: (Heb.) white
LACHLAN: (Celt.) probably derived from 'Laochail', meaning warlike; other references give this as by the sea or inlet
LADO: (Span.) artistic
LAIRD: (Celt.) landed proprietor
LAJOS: (Hung.) famed
LALIT: (Hin.) beautiful
LAMAR: (Fr.-Ger.) the water
LAMBERT: (Teut.) compound of two words meaning land and bright; other authorities give this as both his country's glory and illustrious with landed possessions
LAMONT: (Old Nor.) law-man
LANCE: abbreviation of Lancelot
LANCELOT: (It.) a little lance; (Lat.) he who serves
LANDERS: (Teut.) son of a rural dweller
LANDIS: (Teut.) nature
LANDON: (Teut.) dweller on the mill
LANDOR: (Teut.) country-dweller
LANDRY: (Teut.) lord of the manor
LANE: (Teut.) a passageway
LANGDON: (Teut.) dweller at the long hill

LANGFORD: (Teut.) dweller at the long ford
LANGLEY: (Teut.) dweller at the long meadow
LANN: (Celt.) a sward
LARAMIE: (Fr.) pensive
LARIS: (Lat.) cheerful
LARKIN: (Lat.) laurel
LARRY: a contraction of Laurence
LARS: (Etruscan) lord
LATHA(A)M: (Teut.-Ang.-Sax.) of the village
LATIF: (Arab.) gentle
LATIMER: (Teut.) an interpreter
LAUNCELOT: a variant of Lancelot
LAURENCE, LAWRENCE: (Lat.) laurel; crowned with laurel
LAURIE: a contraction of Laurence or Lawrence
LAVERNE: (Lat.) flourishing
LAWLOR: (Teut.) law-lord
LAWTON: (Old Eng.) a man of refinement
LAZAR: (Heb.) God will help
LEA: (Lat.) a meadow
LEAL: (Lat.) loyal
LEALAND: (Teut.) meadow-land
LEANDER: (Gr.) lion-like
LEAR: (Celt.) calf-keeper; (Teut.) joyful
LEAVITT: (Ice.) a heritage
LEDGARD: (Teut.) national protector
LEDWIN: (Teut.) the nation's friend
LEE: (Teut.-Ang.-Sax.) a shelter, sheltered; also a variant of Lea – a meadow
LEGER: (Teut.) the people's defending spear
LEHMAN: (Teut.) a feudal tenant
LEIF: (Old Nor.) descendant; heir
LEIGH: a variant of Lea
LEIGHTON: (Teut.) dweller in a garden of herbs
LEITH: (Scottish) possibly a place name based on (Gael.) grey
LELAND: (Ang.-Sax.) meadowland; from the meadowlands
LEMUEL: (Heb.) God's own

LENNO: (N.A. Ind.) man
LENNON: (Irish) renowned
LENNOX, LENOX: (Gael.) chieftain
LENUS: (Lat.) mild
LEO: (Lat.-Gr.) lion
LEOFWIN: (Ang.-Sax.) dear friend
LEON: (Gr.) of lion nature
LEONARD: (Gr.) strong and brave as a lion
LEONARDO: (It.) lion-hearted
LEONIDAS: (Gr.) lion-like
LEOPOLD: (Teut.) bold for the people
LEROY: (Old Fr.) the king
LESLIE: (Teut.) one who leases
LESTER: (Ang.-Sax.) shining
LEVANDER: (Old Fr.) an easterly wind blowing off the Mediterranean
LEVI: (Arab.) priest; (Heb.) a concord
LEVIN: (Ang.-Sax.) valued friend
LEWIS: (Teut.) famous warrior; a name popular in Wales
LIAM: (Teut.) protection, will, desire; (Heb.) my people
LINCOLN: (Eng.) lake settlement
LINDEN: (Teut.) gentle
LINDHURST: (Teut.) tranquil wood
LINDLEY: (Teut.) dweller in the tranquil meadow
LINDO: (Teut.) lime tree; (Lat.) handsome
LINDSAY, LINDSEY: (Teut.) of gentle speech
LINFRED: (Teut.) of gentle grace
LINGARD: (Teut.) gentle guard; (Celt.) the sea guard
LINUS: (Heb.) flaxen-haired
LINWOOD: (Eng.) lime wood
LIONEL: (Lat.) young lion
LISLE: (Lat.) from the isle
LLEUFER: (Wel.) splendid
LLEWELLYN: (Celt.) lightning; (Cymric) the lighting sovereign
LLOYD: (Celt.) grey
LLYN: (Cymric) by the sea

LOCHINVAR: (Gael.) origin obscure, but probably some Scottish lake
LOGAN: (Old Eng.) a rocking stone
LOK: (Chin.) happiness
LOMBARD: (Ang.-Sax.) a long beard
LONO: (Haw.) god of peace
LORCAN: (Gael.) fierce in battle
LOREDO: (Lat.) learned
LORENZO: (see Laurence)
LORIMER: (Lat.) maker of bridles
LORING: (Lat.) instructive
LORNE: (Gael.) bereft; forlorn
LORUS: (Lat.) laurel
LORY: (Malayan) a species of parrot
LOT: (Heb.) a covering veil; (Celt.) lion
LOTHARIO: (Teut.) famous warrior
LOUIE: (Teut.) war; fame
LOUIS: a French form of Lewis
LOVEL: (Teut.) a young wolf
LOVELACE: (Old Eng.) a love token
LOVELL: (Teut.) wolf
LOVICK: (Ang.-Sax.) beloved ruler
LOWELL: (Teut.) dweller by the low spring
LOY: (Chin.) open
LUBIN: (Teut.) a beloved friend
LUCA: (Gr.) man from Lucania
LUCAN: (Irish) place of elms
LUCANO: (Lat.) sunrise
LUCAS: (see Lucian)
LUCIAN, LUCIEN: (Lat.) light
LUCIUS: (Lat.) light bringer
LUDLOW: (Teut.) lowly man
LUDWIG: (Teut.) famous warrior
LUIS: Spanish form of Louis
LUKE: a variant of Lucas and Lucian
LUMAN: (Lat.) radiant
LUPE: (Lat.) wolf
LUTHER: (Gr.) illustrious warrior

LYCURGUS: (Gr.) the work of light
LYDELL: (Gr.) a Lydian; pertaining to Lydia in Asia Minor
LYLE: English dialectical contraction of little; (Teut.) an island
LYMAN: (Ang.-Sax.) splendour; man of splendour
LYN: (Ang.-Sax.) a torrent or cascade
LYNDELL: (Teut.) dweller by the cascade in the dell
LYNDON: (Teut.) dweller on a hill beside the castle
LYNFA: (Wel.) place of the lake
LYSANDER: (Gr.) liberator of men
LYULF: (Scan.) fiery wolf

M

MAC: (Gael.) son of
MACAH: (Heb.) one who is like Jehovah
MACAIRE: (Gr.) happy
MACARIO: (Span.) blessed
MACAULEY: (Gael.) son of the phantom
MACKENZIE: (Scottish) son of Kenneth
MACNAIR: (Gael.) son of the heir
MACY: (Old Eng.) sceptre bearer
MADDEN: (Irish) descendant of the hound
MADDOCK, MADOC: (Celt.) fire; (Wel.) goodly; advantaged
MADDOX: (Cymric) force
MADISON: (Teut.) mighty in battle
MAELGWYN: (Wel.) metal-chief
MAGAN: (Teut.) power
MAGNA: (N.A. Ind.) the coming moon
MAGNUS: (Lat.) great
MAHESH: (Hin.) great ruler
MAHMUD: (Arab.) praiseworthy
MAHON: (Celt.) chief
MAHONEY: (Irish) bear
MAITLAND: (Teut.) dweller in the meadowland; (Old Eng.) of the plains or meadows

MAKANI: (Haw.) wind
MAKO: (Heb.) God is with us
MAL(L)ORY: (Lat.-Old Fr.) unfortunate, luckless
MALACHI: (Heb.) God's messenger
MALCHUS: (Heb.) king
MALCOLM: (Gael.) servant or disciple of Colomb
MALISE: (Gael.) servant of God, a disciple of Jesus
MALLARD: (Teut.) strong in counsel
MALONE: (Irish) follower of St John
MALVIN: (Gael.) smooth brow; (Celt.) chief
MANCHU: (Chin.) pure
MANDEL: (Old Fr.) a mantle
MANDER: (Old Fr.) stable-boy
MANFRED: (Teut.) man of peace
MANNIX: (Gael.) little monk
MANOAH: (Heb.) repose
MANOC: (Heb.) great
MANSEL(L): (Wel.) a Norman place name
MANUEL: (see Emmanuel)
MANUS: (Heb.) man at large; the public
MARC: (Heb.) bitter
MARCEL: (Lat.) of warlike qualities
MARCIUS: (Lat.) martial; belonging to Mars
MARCUS: (see Marcius)
MARIUS: (Lat.) of Mars; a disciplinarian
MARK: English form of Marcius
MARLAND: (Teut.) wasteland
MARLEY: (Eng.) pleasant wood
MARLON: (Eng.) origins uncertain; possibly a variant of Marc or Merlin
MARLOW: (Eng.) place name meaning land of the former pool
MARMADUKE: (Celt.) leader at sea; (Ang.-Sax.) a great noble
MARMION: (Gael.) sparkling fame
MAROON: (Teut.) famous master
MARSDEN: (Teut.) valley

of the combat; (Ang.-Sax) from the marsh valley

MARSHAL(L): (Teut.) horse-servant

MARTEL: (Old Fr.) war-hammer

MARTEN: (Lat.) bearer of the sable

MARTIAL: (Lat.) pertaining to Mars, the god of war; warlike

MARTIN: (see Marcius)

MARVIN: (Teut.) warrior friend or famous friend

MASKA: (N.A. Ind.) powerful

MASON: (Teut.) a worker in stone; (Wel.) youth

MAT(T): an abbreviation of Matthew and Matthias

MATH: (Wel.) treasure

MATTHEW, MATTHIAS: (Heb.) gift of Jehovah

MAURICE: (Lat.) a Moor, Moorish

MAX: (see Maximilian)

MAXIM: (Lat.) a premise, serving as a rule or guide

MAXIMILIAN: (Lat.) the greatest Emilius (Aemilianus); often abbreviated to Max

MAXWELL: (Teut.) dweller by the big spring; some authorities give this as a variant of Maximilian

MAYER: (Old Eng.) one who goes a-maying

MAYNARD: (Teut.) hardy strength, might

MAYNE: (Teut.) mighty

MAYO: (Ang.-Sax.) kinsman

MEADE: (Teut.) a strong draught

MEDWIN: (Teut.) strong or worthy friend

MEIR: (Heb.) light-giving

MELBOURNE: (Lat.) favourable destiny

MELCHIOR: (Heb.) King of Light

MELDON: (Lat.) a favourable or pleasant gift

MELFORD: (Gr.) the ford by the mill

MELLIS: (Celt.) disciple of Jesus

MELVA: (Celt.) chief

MELVERN: (N.A. Ind.) great chief

MELVILLE: (Celt.) chief of the people
MELVIN: (Celt.) chief; a variant of Melva
MEMPHIS: (Gr.) beautiful; established
MERCER: (Lat.) merchant
MEREDITH: (Celt.) coast-guard, sea protector
MERGUS: (Lat.) a diver
MERIVALE: modern usage
MERLE: (Teut.) a blackbird
MERLIN: (Celt.) a hill by the sea
MERRICK: (Teut.) renowned ruler
MERRILL: (Teut.) famous
MERTON: (Ang.-Sax.) from near the sea
MERVIN, MERVYN: (Celt.) raven of the sea
MERWIN, MERWYN: (Ang.-Sax.) famous friend
METHUSELAH: (Heb.) man of; used in sixteenth-eighteenth centuries
METIS: (Gr.) a counsellor
MEYER: (Teut.) steward
MICAH: (Heb.) who is like Jehovah; form of Michael
MICHAEL: (Heb.) one who is like the Lord; godly
MICK, MIKE: contractions of Michael
MIGUEL: Spanish form of Michael
MILBURN: (Old Eng.) of the stream by the mill
MILES: (Lat.) a soldier
MILFORD: (Teut.) dweller by the mill by the ford
MILLARD: (Ang.-Sax.) miller
MILLER: (Eng.) practical
MILTON: (Teut.) mill town
MILWARD: (Teut.) mill-keeper
MIRO: (Slav.) peace
MIRSAB: (Arab.) judicious
MISHA: Russian variant of Michael
MITCHELL: (Teut.) a small loaf of bread
MODI: (Nor.) son of the god Thor
MODRED: (Ang.-Sax.) brave advisor
MOE: (Heb.) God's helmet
MOELWYN: (Wel.) fair-haired

MOHAMMAD, MOHAMMED, MUHAMMAD: (Arab.) praiseworthy
MONACO: (Lat.) solitary
MONROE: (Celt.) dweller by the red morass; derived from Mont Roe, on the River Roe in Ireland
MONTAGUE: (Old Eng.) from 'Mont Aigu'
MONTE: (Lat.) a mountain
MONTGOMERY: (Lat.) huntsman
MONTROSE: (Lat.-Eng.) rose of the mountain
MORAG: (Gael.) the sun
MORAY: (Celt.) original form of Murray
MORDAUNT: (Lat.) biter
MORDECAI: (Heb.) combative
MORDEYRN: (Wel.) great monarch
MORELAND: (Teut.) dweller by the moorland
MORELL, MORRELL: (Lat.-Teut.) dark, swarthy
MORGAN: (Teut.) sea-born; seaman
MORICE: a variant of Maurice
MORITZ: (Lat.) dark-skinned; Moorish
MORLEY: (Teut.) dweller by the meadow
MORPHEUS: (Gr.) shape
MORRIS: (Lat.) a moor
MORTIMER: (Celt.) sea-warrior
MORTON: (Ang.-Sax.) from the moor village
MORVEN: (Celt.) seaman
MORYS: a Welsh form of Maurice
MOSES: (Egyp.) drawn out of the water; (Gr.) drawn from the water; (Heb.) the rescued servant of God
MOSTYN: (Wel.) field fortress
MUNGO: (Gael.) amiable
MUNRO, MUNROSE: (see Monroe)
MUNROE: modern usage; (see Monroe)
MURDOCH, MURDOCK: (Gael.) sea man
MURPHY: (Celt.) sea-warrior

MURRAY: (Celt.) a seaman
MUSTAFA: (Arab.) chosen
MYLES: a variant of Miles or Mills
MYLOR: (Celt.) prince
MYLOS: (Slav.) kind
MYRON: (Gr.) fragrant

N

NAAMAN(N): (Heb.) agreeable; pleasant one
NABIL: (Arab.) of noble birth
NADA: (Sans.) thunder; aware
NADABB: (Heb.) he of broad ideas
NADIM: (Arab.) drinking companion
NADIR: (Arab.) rare man
NAHUM: (Heb.) consoling
NAKIA: (Arab.) pure
NALA: (Sans.) legendary king
NALDO: (Teut.) the valiant one
NAMAN: (Sans.) a name
NAMED: (Arab.) the praised
NANDOR: (Hung.) adventurer; form of Fernando
NAPIER: (Gr.) of the new city
NAPOLEON: (Gr.-Lat.) one who belongs to the new city
NARCISSUS: (Gr.) daffodil; in mythology a youth enamoured with his own image
NASH: (Eng.) at the ash tree
NASIR: (Arab.) helper
NAT: abbreviation of Nathan, Nathanael, and Nathaniel
NATHAN: (Heb.) a gift
NATHANAEL, NATHANIEL: (Heb.) God has given
NAVEEN: (Hin.) new
NEAL, NEIL: (Celt.) chief, champion; variants of Nigel
NED: (see Edward)
NEEDHAM: (Teut.) home tyrant
NEHEMIAH: (Heb.) comfort of Jehovah
NEILL: (see Neal)

NELSON: (Eng.) son of Neil
NEMO: (Gr.) grove
NENNOG: (Wel.) heavenly one
NEO: (Lat.) new
NEPHI: (Gr.) cloud
NERO: (Lat.) strong; stern
NESTOR: (Gr.) he who remembers
NETTS: (N.A. Ind.) trusted friend
NEVAN: (Cr.) a name
NEVILLE: (Lat.) of the new city
NEVIN: (Gael.) little saint
NEVLIN: (Celt.) sailor
NEWBERN: (Teut.) new chief
NEWBOLD: (Old Eng.) of the new building
NEWCOMB: (Ang.-Sax.) a stranger
NEWLIN: (Teut.) new arrival
NEWTON: (Ang.-Sax.) of the new town or estate
NIAL(L): (Celt.) champion
NICANDER: (Gr.) man of victory
NICHOLAS, NICOLAS: (Gr.) victor of the people
NICK, NICKY: contractions of Nicholas, Nicolas
NICO: (Gr.) victory
NICODEMUS: (Gr.) the people's victor
NICOMEDE: (Gr.) victorious ruler
NIGEL: origin obscure, but probably Irish; thought to mean dark
NIGER: (Lat.) black
NIKE: (Gr.) winning
NIKITA: (Gr.) unconquered
NILS: a Scandinavian form of Neil
NIMROD: (Heb.) fiery red
NINIAN: (Celt.-Lat.) thought to be a corruption of Vivian; formerly in use in Scotland
NOAH: (Heb.) long rest; consolation
NOAM: (Heb.) joy; delight; pleasantness
NODAS: (Heb.) noble son of the Lord
NODIN: (N.A. Ind.) wind
NOEL: (Old Eng.) the nativity; born on Christmas Day

NOLAN(D): (Gael.) noble
NORBERT: (Teut.) divine brightness
NORMAN: (Old Eng.) a man from the north; (Scan.) divine man
NORRIS: (Teut.) north king
NORTON: (Ang.-Sax.) from the north place or part
NORUA: (Teut.) divine strength
NORVEL: (Fr.) from the northern city
NORVIN: (Teut.) man from the north
NORWOOD: (Teut.) literally, north wood; dweller at the north gate or forest
NOTOS: (Gr.) the south wind
NOVA: (Lat.) new
NOWELL: (Teut.) variant of Noel
NUNO: (Lat.) ninth; the ninth child
NUNZIO: (It.) messenger

O

OAKLEY: (Teut.-Ang.-Sax.) dweller at the oak meadow
OBADIAH: (Heb.) serving the Lord
OBAMA: (African) crooked
OBED: (Heb.) serving; worshipper (of God)
OBERON: (Teut.) royal bear
OBERT: (Teut.) illustrious
OCTAVIUS, OCTAVOS: (Lat.) eighth; eighth son
ODA: (Heb.) praise God
ODAGOMA: (N.A. Ind.) iron nerve
ODAKOTA: (N.A. Ind.) one with many friends
ODALRIC: (Teut.) rich ruler
ODEL, ODELL: (Nor.) man of a rich estate
ODELON: (Teut.) rich; wealth
ODIC: (Gr.) a song or ode
ODIN: (Scan.) Norse god of magic
ODMAR: (Teut.) rich man of fame

ODMUND: (Teut.) rich protector
ODO: (Teut.) rich
ODOLF: (Teut.) wise rich man
ODON: (Teut.) rich master
ODWIN: (Teut.) rich friend
OGDEN: (Ang.-Sax.) from the oak valley
OGILVIE, OGILVY: (Celt.) high peak
OGMUND: (Teut.) awesome protector
OHIN: (Jap.) wanted child
OLA: (Heb.) eternity
OLAF: (Teut.) ancestor's relic; a name adopted by Swedish kings
OLAVE: (Nor.) ancestor's relic
OLCOTT: (Teut.) dweller in the old cottage
OLEANDER: (Haw.) joyous
OLEG: (Rus.) holy
OLEN: (Teut.) inheritor
OLIVER: (Lat.) the olive or olive tree, suggesting peace
OLMOS: (Span.) altruistic
OLVIDIO (Span.) forgetful
OMAN: (Scan.) high protector
OMANISA: (N.A. Ind.) wanderer
OMAR: (see Umar)
ONAN: (Turk.) wealthy
ONDA: (It.) wave
ONESIMUS: (Gr.) beneficial
ONLLWYN: (Wel.) ash-grove
ONORATO: (Lat.) honoured
ONSLOW: (Old Eng.) hill of the zealous one
OPIE: (Gr.) opium
ORAN: (Irish) a wren; sometimes used in Ireland for Adrian
ORBAN: (Lat.) citizen
OREL: (Lat.) the listener
OREN: (Heb.) the pine tree
ORIEN: (Lat.) sunrise
ORLANDO: an Italian form of Roland
ORLAY: (Span.) famed
ORLI, ORLY: (Heb.) light is mine
ORLIN: (Gr.-Lat.) golden brightness
ORLON: (Teut.) rich
ORMOND: (Teut.) famous protector

ORO: (It.) gold
ORPHEUS: (Gr.) beautiful voice
ORRA: origin unknown; unmatched; odd
ORRICK: (Teut.) golden rule
ORRIN: (Eng.) boy of the river
ORRIS: (Old Fr.) a certain kind of gold or silver lace
ORSINO: (Lat.) bear-like; superior qualities
ORSON: a variant of Orsino
ORTENSIO: (Lat.) gardener
ORTWIN: (Teut.) rich friend
ORVILLE: (Old Fr.) lord of the estate; (man of) the rich town
ORWIN: (Teut.) golden friend
OSBERT: (Teut.) brightness of a god
OSBORN: (Teut.) sacred bear; (Old Eng.) godly bear
OSCAR: (Celt.) bounding warrior
OSFRED: (Teut.) divine power
OSGOOD: (Teut.) divinely good
OSLAC: (Teut.) divine sport
OSMER: (Teut.) divinely famed
OSMOND: (Teut.) protected by God
OSRIC: (Teut.) divine ruler
OSWALD: (Teut.) divine power
OSWIN: (Ang.-Sax.) divine friend
OSWYTH: (Teut.) divine strength
OTADAN: (N.A. Ind.) plenty
OTIS: (Gr.) keen hearing
OTTE: (Teut.) happy
OTTO: (Teut.) rich; a variant of Odo
OTWAY, OTTWAY: (Teut.) lucky warrior
OTWEL: (Teut.) instrument of dread
OURAY: (N.A. Ind.) an arrow
OUTRAM: (Teut.) honoured warrior
OWEN: (Celt.) warrior; (Lat.) well-born

OZ: (Heb.) strength
OZUL: (Heb.) a shadow

P

PABLO: (Span.) little
PACIAN: (Lat.) man of peace
PACO: (N.A. Ind.) bold eagle
PADARN: (Wel.) fatherly
PADDY: a contraction of Patrick
PADMA: (Sans.) flower of the lotus
PADRAIG: (Irish) noble; form of Patrick
PAGET: (Old Fr.) little page; associated with pageantry
PAGIEL: (Heb.) worships
PAINE: (Lat.) man of the country
PAISLEY: (Lat.) yield of the country
PAKAVI: (N.A. Ind.) a reed
PALLADIN: (Gr.) wise; confrontational
PALLATON: (N.A. Ind.) fighter
PALMA: (Lat.) successful
PALMER: (Lat.-Ang.-Sax.) pilgrim
PANOS: (Gr.) all holy
PAOLO: (Lat.) a little stone
PAPILLION: (Fr.) butterfly
PARIS: (Gr.) the son of the king of Troy
PARK: (Chin.) the cypress tree
PARKER: (Teut.) keeper of a park
PARR: (Eng.) protective
PARRY: (Lat.) equality
PASCAL: (Heb.) deliverance; Easter or Passover child
PASCOE: an English variant of Pascal
PAT: a contraction of Patrick
PATE: (Gael.) noble; (Eng.) crown of the head; a Scottish version of Patrick
PATERA: (Sans.) a bird
PATRICK: (Lat.) patrician; nobleman
PATTEN: (Eng.) noble
PATTRA: (Sans.) pinion of a wing
PATU: (Sans.) a protector

PATWIN: (N.A. Ind.) a man
PAUL: (Lat.) small; an English form of Paulus
PAULUS: (Lat.) small
PAVEL: (Lat.) small
PAWLEY: an old English variant of Paul
PAX: (Lat.) peace
PAXTON: (Teut.) a traveller from a distant part
PAYNE: (Lat.) rustic
PAYTON: (Ang.-Sax.) St Patrick's town
PEARSON: (Eng.) dark-eyed
PEDRO: a Spanish form of Peter
PELEG: (Heb.) a division
PELEX: (Gr.) a warrior's helmet
PELHAM: (Eng.) Peola's place
PENDLETON: (Cymric) derived from an English town named after its rock outcrops
PENN: (Ang.-Sax.) enclosure
PENROD: (Wel.) top of the ford
PENROSE: (Celt.) one who lives at the head of the moor; an English place name
PENWYN: (Wel.) fair head
PEPIN: (Teut.) ardent
PERCIVAL: (Fr.) pierce the valley; (Gr.) courteous
PERCY: a diminutive of Percival
PEREGRINE: (Lat.) stranger; pilgrim traveller
PEREZ: (Heb.) breach
PERICLES: (Gr.) famed far and wide
PERKIN: (Eng.) opinionated
PERRY: (Eng.) based on the Latin meaning stranger; also a contraction of Peregrine
PERSEUS: (Gr.) destroyer; fabled Greek hero who slew Medusa
PETER: (Lat.-Gr.) a rock
PETROS: (Gr.) of stone
PEVERIL: (Lat.) boyish
PHAO: (Gr.) giver of light
PHAON: (Gr.) brilliant
PHARAMOND: (Teut.) journey protection
PHARAOH: (Egyp.) the sun

PHARIS: (Irish) heroic
PHAROS: (Gr.) a beacon
PHELAN: (Celt.) wolf; sometimes considered a good luck omen
PHELIM: (Celt.) good
PHILANDER: (Gr.) a man who loves all mankind
PHILARET: (Gr.) a lover of virtue
PHILEMON: (Gr.) a kiss; loving
PHILETAS, PHILETUS: (Gr.) beloved
PHILIBERT: (Teut.) very bright
PHILIP: (Gr.) a lover of horses
PHILO: (Gr.) love
PHINEAS: (Heb.) mouth of brass
PHOEBUS: (Gr.) the shining one
PHOENIX: (Gr.) dark red
PIERCE: modern usage
PIERRE: French form of Peter
PIERREPONT: (Fr.) stone bridge
PIERS: an early English form of Peter
PIERSON: (Fr.) son of Pierre
PIUS: (Lat.) dutiful
PLATO: (Gr.) broad; broad-shouldered; name of famous Greek philosopher
PLAUDO: (Lat.) one who is worthy of praise; applauded
POLDO: (Teut.) the people's prince
POLLARD: (Tent.) the unafraid
POMROY: (Lat.) apple king; (Old Fr.) apple orchard
PORTER: (Eng.) gatekeeper
POWA: (N.A. Ind.) rich
POWELL: (Celt.) alert
POWYS: (Wel.) a man from Powis
PRADEEP: (Hin.) light
PRESCOTT: (Ang.-Sax.) the priest's house
PRESLEY: (Old Eng.) priest's meadow
PRESTON: (Ang.-Sax.) the priest's village
PRICE: (Wel.) son of Rhys
PRIMA: (Sans.) beloved
PRIMUS: (Lat.) first
PROBERT: (Teut.) brilliance

PROBUS: (Lat.) honest
PROCTOR: (Lat.) leader
PROSPER, PROSPERO: (Lat.) prosperous
PROTEUS: (Gr.) changeful
PRYOR: (Eng.) first
PURDY: (Hin.) a recluse
PURVANCE: (Slav.) the first
PWYLL: (Wel.) prudence
PYTHIAS: (Gr.) the inquiring

Q

QUADIM: (Arab.) able
QUAID: (Irish) fourth
QUARTUS: (Lat.) fourth; the fourth son
QUENTIN: (Lat.) fifth; the fifth son
QUERON: (Celt.) black or dark
QUIGLEY: (Irish) nature-loving
QUILLAN: (Gael.) sword
QUILLER: (Teut.) a fledgling
QUINCY: (Teut.) a dialectic form of whence; (Fr.) a place name
QUINLAN: (Irish) well-formed one
QUINN: (Gael.) counsel
QUINTON: a variant of Quentin
QUITO: (Span.) lively
QUONG: (Chin.) bright

R

RAB: (Teut.) bright fortune
RADBERT: (Teut.) bright counsellor
RADCLIFFE: (Teut.) red cliff
RADFORD: (Eng.) dweller by the swift water ford
RADLEY: (Old Eng.) red meadow
RADMAN: (Slav.) joy
RADNOR: (Eng.) natural; child of the bright shore
RAE: (Teut.) a roe
RAFAEL: (see Raphael)
RAFE: a phonetic form of Ralph
RAFI: (Arab.) musical
RAGMAR: (Teut.) wise warrior

RAGNOLD: (Teut.) powerful judge
RAHEEM: (Arab.) merciful; kind
RAHM: (Heb.) pleasing
RAINER: (Teut.) prudent warrior
RAJ, RAJA: (Sans.) king
RALEIGH: (Teut.) dweller at the roe meadow; (Eng.) from the hunting lodge
RALPH: (Old Eng.) from word Raedwulf, a compound of counsel and wolf, which became Radulf and then Ralf; (Teut.) house wolf; also probably a contraction of Randolf
RAMA: (Sans.) bringer of joy
RAMAH: (Heb.) a lofty place; (Lat.) a brand
RAMBERT: (Teut.) bright raven
RAMIRO: (Teut.) strong in battle
RAMON: (Teut.) protecting judge
RAMSAY, RAMSEY: (Teut.) the strong
RAMSDEN: (Eng.) valley of the rams
RANA: (Sans.) prince
RANALD: (Teut.) powerful counsel; a variant of Ronald
RANDAL: a variant of Randolf
RANDER: (Teut.) home-lover
RANDOLF, RANDOLPH: (Teut.) house-wolf
RANI: (Heb.) joyful
RANNOCH: (Gael.) fern
RANSOME: (Middle Eng.) redemption
RAOUL: (Teut.) helpful commander
RAPHAEL: (Heb.) God has healed
RASHAD: (Arab.) good judgment
RASMUS: form of Erasmus – the desired
RATHBONE: (Old Fr.) dweller at the river fort
RATHBURN: (Teut.) dweller at the running brook
RAVELIN: (Lat.) a rampart
RAVI: (Fr.) delighted

RAWDON: (Teut.) a red roe
RAY: contraction of Raymond
RAYMOND: (Teut.) wise or good protector
RAYNALD: (Teut.) of firm judgment
RAYNOR: (Teut.) wise or discreet warrior
RAYO: (Teut.) a beam of light
READ, READE: (Teut.) ruddy; red-haired
REAGAN: (Irish) little king
REBA: (Heb.) a quarter
REDMOND: (Teut.) protecting counsellor
REECE: (Teut.) swift; an English form of Rhys
REEVE, REEVES: (Old Eng.) high official of a district; a bailiff or steward
REGAN: (Celt.) royal; king
REGINALD: (see Reynold)
REGULUS: (Lat.) a little king
REID: (Old Eng.) by the reeds
REILLY: (Eng.) brave
REINALDO: (Teut.) pure and brave
REINGARD: (Teut.) incorruptible guard
REINHART: (Teut.) of incorruptible firmness; staunch
REMUS: (Lat.) fair
REMY: (Lat.) an oarsman
RENARD: (Teut.) of firm decision
RENATO: (Lat.) rebirth
RENAUD: (Old Fr.) powerful judgment
RENAULD: (Lat.) reborn
RENÉ: (Fr.) reborn
RENFRED: (Teut.) wise and peaceful judgment
REUBEN: (Heb.) renewer; a child that has taken the place of one that has died
REUEL: (Heb.) friend of God
REVEL: (Heb.) a shepherd; (Lat.) joy
REX: (Lat.) king
REXFORD: (Teut.) from the king's ford
REXWALD: (Teut.) of kingly power

REYBURN: (Teut.) a flaming way
REYHAN: (Arab.) the favoured of a deity
REYNER: (Lat.) kingly
REYNOLD: (Lat.-Teut.) regal judgment, power and might
REZON: (Heb.) prince
RHAIN: (Wel.) a lance
RHESA: (Chaldaic) prince
RHODES: (Gr.) roses
RHODRI: (Wel.) ruler of the circle
RHONWEN: (Wel.) slender and fair
RHUN: (Wel.) grand
RHYS: (Celt.) a chief
RICHARD: (Teut.) harsh king; an Old Eng. compound of ruler and hard
RICHMOND: (Teut.) the protecting ruler
RIDDELL: (Old Eng.) a sieve
RIDLEY: (Teut.) dweller on the dark ridge; (Old Eng.) dweller by the red field
RIGBY: (Old Eng.) farm on a ridge
RILEY: (Old Eng.) turbid; disorderly
RIMMON: (Heb.) thunderer
RIO: (Span.) river
RIORDAN: (Celt.) royal bard
RITCHIE: (Teut.) firm ruler
RIZO: (It.) lively
ROALD: (Teut.) famed power
ROARKE: (Gael.) famous ruler
ROB: (see Robert)
ROBERT: (Teut.) bright flame
ROBIN: Scottish diminutive of Robert
ROCCO: (It.) repose
RODERIC, RODERICK: (Teut.) rich in fame
RODGER: (Teut.) praise
RODMUND: (Teut.) famous protector
RODNEY: (Teut.) famous
RODOLPH: (Teut.) hero; wolf
ROGER: (see Rodger)
ROHIN: (Sans.) one who follows the upward path

ROLAND: (Teut.) fame of the land
ROLF: a variant of Rudolph
ROLLIE: (Teut.) renowned land
ROLLO: (see Rodolph)
ROMAN: (Rus.) man from Rome
ROMEO: (It.) a pilgrim to Rome
ROMERO: (Lat.) a wanderer
ROMNEY: (Wel.) roamer
ROMOLO: (Teut.) fame
RONAK: (Scan.) powerful
RONALD: (Teut.) powerful counsel; Scottish equivalent of Reynold and Reginald
RONAN: (Gael.) little seal
RONDELL: (It.) plump, round
RORY: (Celt.) red
ROSCOE: (Teut.) sea-horse
ROSPERT: (Teut.) bright horse
ROSS: (Teut.) a horse
ROSSER: (Celt.) champion
ROVER: (Eng.) wanderer
ROWAN: (Celt.) famous
ROWE: (Ang.-Sax.) rest
ROWLAND: (see Roland)
ROY: (Celt.) red
ROYCE, ROYSTON: (Teut.) royal
ROYDEN: (Teut.) dweller in the king's glen
RUBIN: (Lat.) a ruby
RUDOLPH: (see Rodolph)
RUFORD, RUFFORD: (Old Eng.) of the red ford
RUFUS: (Lat.) red; red-haired
RULAND: (Teut.) famed in the land
RULIFF: (Teut.) fortunate
RUPERT: (See Robert)
RUSSELL: (Teut.) the fox
RYAN: (Lat.) laughing
RYDER: (Eng.) horseman
RYLAN: (Eng.) place where rye is grown

S

SAADI: (Pers.) wise
SABAS: (Heb.) rest
SABIAN: (Heb.) host of heaven
SABINE: (Lat.) a tribal name

SABU: (Hin.) follower of a tribe
SACHA, SASHA: (Rus.) variant of Alexander
SAD: (Celt.) the just
SADOC: (Heb.) sacred
SAHALE: (N.A. Ind.) above
SAID: (Arab.) happy; lucky
SAIRE: (Teut.) hermit
SAKARI: (N.A. Ind.) sweet
SAKIMA: (N.A. Ind.) king
SALADIN: (Arab.) goodness of the faith
SALAH: (Arab.) goodness; righteousness
SALIM: (Arab.) safe, secure
SALVADOR: (Lat.) saviour
SAMA: (Sans.) tranquillity
SAMIR: (Arab.) pleasant companion
SAMSON, SAMPSON: (Heb.) splendid sun
SAMUEL: (Heb.) heard of God; in the name of God
SAMULA: (Sans.) foundation
SANCHIA: (Span.) holy
SANCHO: (Lat.) holy
SANDFORD: (Ang.-Sax.) a sandy ford or crossing
SANFRED: (Teut.) peaceful counsel
SANJAY: (Sans.) triumphant
SANSON: (Heb.) brilliant sun
SANUYA: (N.A. Ind.) cloud
SAPATA: (N.A. Ind.) hugging bear
SARID: (Heb.) a survivor
SAUL: (Heb.) longed for; asked of God
SAVA: (Heb.) repose
SAVERO: (Arab.) bright
SAWA: (N.A. Ind.) rock
SAXON: (Teut.) rock; (Ang.-Sax.) short-sword warrior
SAYRES: (Teut.) conquering host
SCHOLEM: (Heb.) peace
SCHUYLER: (Dutch) a place of shelter; a shelterer
SCIPIO: (Lat.) a staff
SCOTT: modern usage
SEADON: (Old Eng.) one who lives in the field near the sea
SEAFORTH: (Teut.) peaceful conqueror
SEAMUS: Irish variant of James

SEAN, SHAWN: an Irish form of John – Jehovah has favoured; the Lord graciously giveth
SEARLE, SEARLES: (Teut.) a wearer of armour
SEATON: (Teut.) one who lives on an estate near the sea
SEAVER: (Ang.-Sax.) of the victorious stronghold
SEBA: (Gr.) venerated
SEBASTIAN: (Gr.) venerable
SEBERT: (Ang.-Sax.) famous in victory
SECUNDO: (Lat.) the second; second son
SEDGWICK: (Ang.-Sax.) sedgy (reedy) village
SEFTON: (Old Eng.) after the place name in England
SEIF: (Arab.) the sword of religion
SELAS: (Gr.) a bright flame
SELBY: (Old Eng.) willow farm
SELDON: (Teut.) rare
SELED: (Heb.) the leaper
SELFRIDGE: (Teut.) lord of the ridge
SELIG, ZELIG: (Teut.) blessed
SELMAR: (Lat.) the rolling sea
SELVAC: (Celt.) rich in cattle
SELWYN: (Ang.-Sax.) blessed friend
SEMA: (Gr.) a sign from heaven
SEPTIMUS: (Lat.) seventh; the seventh child
SERGIO: (Lat.) servant
SERLO: (Teut.) armour
SETH: (Heb.) the appointed
SEVER: (Lat.) austere
SEWARD: (Ang.-Sax.) victory protection; (Teut.) warden of the sea coast
SEWELL: (Ang.-Sax.-Teut.) victorious rule
SEXTUS: (Lat.) sixth; the sixth child
SEYMOUR: (Teut.) the sower
SHALLUM: (Heb.) perfect
SHAMUS: Irish form of James
SHANAHAN: (Celt.) sagacious

SHANE: an Irish form of John
SHANLEY: (Gael.) son of the hero
SHAPONDA: (N.A. Ind.) passing through
SHARIF: (Arab.) honoured
SHAW: (Teut.) from a shady grove
SHAWN: (Heb.) grace of the Lord
SHEA: (Irish) stately; courageous
SHEEAN: (Celt.) courteous
SHELBY: (Nor.) willow
SHELDON: (Teut.) shield-bearer
SHEM: (Heb.) name; renown
SHERARD: (Teut.) splendidly brave
SHERIDAN: (Gael.) wild man
SHERLOCK: (Eng-Teut.) fair-haired; (Middle Eng.) shorn head
SHERMAN: (Ang.-Sax.) a wool shearer
SHERWIN: (Ang.-Sax.) a true friend
SHERWOOD: (Celt.) sea ruler; (Ang.-Sax.) bright forest
SHILOH: (Heb.) His gift
SHIRA: (Heb.) welfare
SHOLA: (Arab.) energetic
SHOLTO: (Celt.) sower
SHOMER: (Heb.) watcher
SIBOLD: (Teut.) conquering prince
SID: (Teut.) conqueror
SIDNEY: (Teut.) of St Denys
SIEBERT: (Teut.) bright conqueror
SIEGFRIED: (Teut.) victorious peace
SIEVER: (Scan.) victorious guard
SIGMUND: (Teut.) victorious protector
SILABU: (N.A. Ind.) a falcon
SILAS: (Lat.) of the forest; god of trees
SILEO: (Teut.) conquering messenger
SILSBY: (Old Eng.) of the forest farm
SILVA: (Lat.) of the forest
SILVESTER: (Lat.)

growing in a wood; forest dweller
SIM, SIMEON: (Heb.) obedient; hearkening
SIMBA: (Arab.) lion
SIMON: a form of Simeon
SINCLAIR: (Lat.) saintly; illustrious
SIRIUS: (Heb.) brightest star
SIVA: (Heb.) propitious
SKELTON: (Old Eng.) farmstead on a hill
SKERRY: (Old Nor.) sea rock
SKIPPER: (Eng.) ship's captain
SLADE: (Eng.) valley
SLOANE: (Celt.) fighter, warrior
SNOWDON: (Eng.) snowy hill
SOFIAN: (Arab.) devoted
SOL: (Lat.) the sun; also a diminutive of Solomon
SOLOMON: (Heb.) man of peace
SOLON: (Gr.) wisdom
SONGAN: (N.A. Ind.) string
SONNY: a variant of Saul or Solomon
SORLE: (Teut.) armour
SPENCER: (Old Eng.) a dispenser (of provisions)
SPIRO: (Gr.) breath of the gods
SPRAGUE: (Dutch) eloquent; (Old Eng.) the alert one
STACY: (Lat.) stable; dependable
STANFIELD: (Ang,-Sax.) stony field
STANFORD: (Ang.-Sax.) stony crossing
STANISLAUS: (Slav.) camp glory
STANLEY: (Teut.) a form of Stanislaus
STARR: (Teut.) inflexible
STATON: (Teut.) of the stone dwelling
STAVROS: (Gr.) crowned
STEIN: (Teut.) stone
STEINHART: (Teut.) stony; unyielding
STELLAN: (Lat.) starred
STEPHEN, STEVEN: (Gr.) a crown
STERLING: (Teut.) true
STEWART, STUART: (Teut.) an administrator

STIG: (Old Nor.) wanderer
STIRLING: (Middle Eng.) little star
STODDARD: (Ang.-Sax.) keeper of horses; (Old. Fr.) a peaceful man
STRACHAN: (Scottish) little valley
STURGES: (Gr.) natural affection; parental love
SULIEN: (Wel.) sun-born
SULLIVAN: (Celt.) blue-eyed
SULWYN: (Wel.) sun-fair
SUTA: (N.A. Ind.) tough
SVEN: (Nor.) boy
SWAIN: (Teut.) a youth in service
SWEYN: (Ang.-Sax.) servant; swineherd
SYDNEY: (Teut.) of St Denys
SYED: (Arab.) lucky
SYENA: (Sans.) hawk, falcon
SYLGWYN: (Wel.) Whitsun
SYLVESTER: (see Silvester)

T

TABOR: (Turk.) a fortified encampment
TADEO: (Aramaic) praise
TADHG: (Irish) poet; philosopher
TAKASHI: (Jap.) praiseworthy
TAKODA: (N.A. Ind.) friend to all
TALBOT: (Old Eng.) name of original stock of blood-hounds, used in heraldic signs
TAMA: (N.A. Ind.) a thunderbolt
TAMIR: (Arab.) tall and wealthy
TARIAN: (Wel.) silver
TARIQ: (Arab.) night star
TARUN: (Hin.) young
TATE: (N.A. Ind.) windy; a great talker
TAYLOR: (Teut.) a cutter of cloth
TEAGUE: (Celt.) poet
TED, TEDDY: contractions of Edward and Theodore

TEDMAN: (Teut.) patriot
TERENCE: (Lat.) tender
TERRY: (Teut.) well-respected ruler; also a contraction of Terence
TERTIUS: (Lat.) three; the third son
TESMOND: (Teut.) a protector from evil
TEVIS: (Old Eng.) a shilling
THADDEUS: (Syriac) wise; (Aramaic) praise
THEO: (see Theodore)
THEOBALD: (Teut.) brave race
THEODORE: (Gr.) divine gift
THEOPHILUS: (Gr.) loved of God
THERON: (Gr.) hunter
THIERRY: French form of Terence
THOMAS: (Aramaic-Heb.) twin
THOR: (Nor.) thunder
THORBERT: (Teut.) Thor's thunder
THORLEY: (Eng.) thorn wood
THORNTON: (Eng.) settlement among the thorns
THOROLD: (Scan.) having power from Thor
THORPE: (Teut.) from a village
THURLOW: (Teut.) Thor's sport; (Celt.) a low tower
THURSTAN, THURSTON: (Teut.) Thor's jewel; (Dan.) stone
TIBAL: (Teut.) people's prince
TIBOR: (Slav.) holy place
TIERNAN: (Celt.) kingly
TIM: a contraction of Timothy
TIMON: (Gr.) honourable
TIMOTHY: (Gr.) compound of honour, respect and a god; (Heb.) God-fearing
TITUS: (Lat.) saved, safe
TOBIAH, TOBIAS: (Heb.) the Lord is good
TOBY: (Heb.) God is good; a contraction of Tobias
TODD: (Eng.) fox
TOM: an English contraction of Thomas

TONY: a contraction of Anthony and Antony
TOOLE: (Celt.) lordly
TORBERT: (Teut.) bright eminence
TORIN: (Gael.) chief
TORQUIL: (Nor.) from the god Thor
TORR: (Old Eng.) from the tower
TRACY, TRACEY: (Old Eng.) a pathway
TRAFFORD: (Lat.-Teut.) dweller beyond the ford
TRAHEARN: (Wel.) iron
TRAVERS: (Old Fr.) athwart
TRAVIS: (Teut.) uniting; (Fr.) crossroads
TREVOR: (Celt.) discreet
TREY: (Eng.) possibly based on the word three
TRISTAN, TRISTRAM: (Celt.) tumult; (Lat.) grave; sorrowful
TROY: (Irish) foot-soldier
TRUMAN: (Old Eng.) trusted man
TUDOR: (Celt.) divine gift
TUDWAL: (Wel.) tribe wall
TURNER: (Eng.) lathe-worker
TYLER: (Eng.) tile-maker
TYNDALL: (Ang.-Sax.) an ever-burning light
TYRONE: (Irish) Owen's land
TYSON: (Teut.) son of the German

U

UDO: (Lat.) humid
UISDEAN: (Old Nor.) always stone; also a variant of Hugh
ULAND: (Teut.) from a noble land
ULRICA: (Nor.) ruler
ULRICK: (Teut.) noble ruler
ULTAN: (Irish) from Ulster
ULTANN: (Wel.) saintly
ULYSSES: (Gr.) the hater
UMAR: (Arab.) populous; flourishing
UNNI: (Heb.) modest
UNO: (Lat.) the one; a name meaning perfection
UNWIN: (Old Eng.) not a friend

UPTON: (Ang.-Sax.) town on the heights
URBAN: (Lat.) of the town
URHO: (Finn.) brave
URI: (Heb.) light
URIAH: (Heb.) light of the Lord
URIEL: (Heb.) angel of light
URIEN: (Wel.) town-born
URLWIN: (Teut.) noble friend
UZI: (Heb.) my power

V

VADIM: a Russian variant of Vladimir
VAL: (see Valentine)
VALDEMAR: (Teut.) renowned leader
VALDIS: (Teut.) lively in battle
VALENTINE: (Lat.) strong; healthy
VALERY: (Teut.) fierce ruler
VAN: (Dutch) noble descent
VANCE: (Old Eng.) fen-dweller
VANGELIS: (Gr.) good news
VANYA: (Rus.) right
VARUN: (Hin.) god of water
VASILIS: (Gr.) king-like
VAUGHAN: (Celt.) little
VENN: (old Eng.) handsome
VERNON: (Lat.) flourishing
VICTOR: (Lat.) conqueror
VIDAL: (Span.) life
VIGGO: (Scan.) exuberant
VIJAY: (Sans.) victory; booty
VIKRAM: (Sans.) heroism; strength
VINCENT: (Lat.) conquering
VIRGIL: (Lat.) flourishing
VITO: (Span.) life
VIVIAN: (Lat.) lively
VLADIMIR: (Slav.) the glory of ruling princes
VOLKER: (Teut.) defender of the people
VOLNEY: (Teut.) popular
VON: (Nor.) hope
VYCHAN: (Wel.) little
VYVIAN, VYVYAN: variants of Vivian

W

WADE: (Dutch) a meadow
WAINRIGHT: (Old Eng.) cart-maker
WALDEMAR: (Teut.) celebrated power
WALDEN: (Teut.) mighty
WALDO: (see Walden)
WALID: (Arab.) newborn baby
WALKER: (Eng.) a fuller
WALLACE: (Lat.) foreigner
WALLY: (Teut.) ruler of the army; also a contraction of Walter
WALSTAN: (Ang.-Sax.) wall-stone; corner-stone
WALTER: (Teut.) powerful
WALTON: (Old Eng.) farmstead of the Britons
WARD: (Teut.) one who keeps guard
WARDELL: (Eng.) watchman's hill
WARNER: (Old Fr.) to guard; (Teut.) protecting warrior
WARREN: (Teut.) a park
WARWICK: (Teut.) camp
WASIM: (Arab.) handsome
WASSILY: (Gr.) kingly
WATSON: (Eng.) son of Walter
WAVERLEY: (Eng.) quaking aspen
WAYLON: (Eng.) land by the road
WAYNE: (Teut.) an ancient wagon
WEBSTER: (Old Eng.) weaver
WENDELL: (Teut.) a wanderer
WESLEY: (see Westley)
WESTLEY: (Ang.-Sax.) of the west meadow
WHITAKER, WHITTAKER: (Old Eng.) white acre
WILBERFORCE: (Old Eng.) Wilbur's ditch
WILBUR: (Teut.) bright resolve
WILDON: (Ang.-Sax.) curving valley
WILEY: (Old Eng.) beguiling; enchanting
WILFRED, WILFRID: (Teut.) resolute peace

WILL: a contraction of William

WILLARD: (Teut.) hardy will

WILLIAM: (Teut.) derived from compound of will and helmet; resolute helmet, defender

WILLIS: (Eng.) Will's servant

WILLOUGHBY: (Old Nor.) from the farm by the willow trees

WILMER: (Teut.) of famous resolution

WILMOT: (Teut.) resolute

WINDSOR: (Old Eng.) riverbank with a windlass

WINSLOW: (Teut.) from the friendly hill

WINSTON: (Teut.) a dweller in a friendly town

WINTHROP: (Ang.-Sax.) from the friendly village

WOLFGANG: (Teut.) the way of the wolves

WOODROW: (Old Eng.) row of houses by a wood

WYATT: (Fr.) a guide

WYNN: (Wel.) white; blessed

WYSTAND: (Ang.-Sax.) battle stone

XANDER: (Gr.) defender of the people

XANTHUS: (Gr.) golden-haired

XAVIER: (Arab.) bright

XENEK: (Gr.) a stranger

XENON: (Gr.) the guest

XENOPHON: (Gr.) strange-sounding

XENOS: (Gr.) strange

XERXES: (Pers.) king

YAHIR: (Span.) handsome one

YALE: (Teut.) one who pays

YANIS: (Gr.) gift from God; form of John

YARDLEY: (Teut.) dweller in the meadow pastures

YATES: (Ang.-Sax.) one who guards the gate
YEHUDI: a variant of Judah
YEMON: (Jap.) guarding the gate
YESTIN: (Wel.) just
YNYR: (Wel.) honour
YONA: (N.A. Ind.) bear; (Heb.) dove
YORICK: (Dan.) variant of George
YORK: (Eng.) yew tree
YVE, YVES: (Fr.) yew tree; **YVES:** (Scan.) an archer
YVON: (Teut.) archer
YWAIN: (Celt.) young warrior

Z

ZABROS: (Gr.) glutton
ZACHARIAS, ZACHARY: (Heb.) remembered of Jehovah
ZADOK: (Heb.) the just
ZAFAR: (Arab.) triumphant
ZAK: a contraction of Zachary
ZANE: (Eng.) possibly a variant of John or derived from a place name
ZARAB: (Sud.) protection against enemies
ZAREK: (Pers.) God protect the king
ZAVIER: (see Xavier)
ZEDEKIAH: (Heb.) righteousness of Jehovah
ZEKE: a contraction of Ezekiel
ZEL: (Pers.) cymbal
ZELIG: (Teut.) blessed
ZELOS: (Gr.) emulation
ZENO: (Gr.) stranger
ZENOS: (Gr.) Jupiter's gift
ZEPHANIAH: (Heb.) hidden from God
ZERAH: (Heb.) a rising light
ZIVAN: (Slav.) lively
ZURIAL: (Heb.) God is my rock